Concise PhraseBook for Writing Academic English

Concise PhraseBook for Writing Academic English
Updated first edition 2023

PhraseBook for Writing Papers and Research in English
Updated fourth edition 2023

Published by The Whole World Company • Cambridge • CB7 5EQ • England

Imprint: Whole World Company Press

© 2023, 2022, 2007, 2002, 2001, 2000 Stephen Howe

Printed in the USA, UK, EU, Australia and other countries/regions (1.4)

The author hereby asserts his moral rights to be identified as the author of the PhraseBook. You may not remove or alter the author's name, publisher's name, copyright notice, disclaimers or any license agreement. Database right The Whole World Company (maker).

PhraseBook for Writing, EnglishforResearch.com, EnglishforStudents.com and EnglishforSchool.com are worldwide trademarks and/or service marks of The Whole World Company Limited. All other trademarks and registered trademarks are the property of their respective owners and are hereby acknowledged.

Do not make illegal, unauthorized copies of the PhraseBook. The PhraseBook and digital versions are protected by copyright law and international treaties. All rights reserved worldwide. Copyright is reserved in English and all other languages and countries of the world.

The publisher and author have striven to ensure the accuracy and correctness of the PhraseBook; however, they can accept no responsibility for any loss or inconvenience as a consequence of use, information or advice contained in the PhraseBook.

ISBN-10: 1 903384 09 5
ISBN-13: 978 1 903384 09 1

EnglishforResearch.com

Contents

Contents iii
About the Concise PhraseBook v
Also available ix
Phrases 13
   1   Preface and acknowledgements 13
   2   Writing a bio 16
   3   Introducing a study or presentation 18
   4   The aim of your study and outlining the topic 20
   5   Defining the scope of your study or presentation 23
   6   Your method or approach 25
   7   Definitions, notation and terminology 29
   8   Presenting data 32
   9   Giving examples 34
  10   Literature review and the relationship to other work 36
  11   Referring to other work 42
  12   Reviewing other work 44
  13   What you agree with 46
  14   What you disagree with 47
  15   Arguing your case and putting forward ideas 51
  16   Arguing against 53
  17   Analysis and discussion 55
  18   Explaining and giving reasons 58
  19   Qualifying and hedging 60
  20   Quantifying 63
  21   Time 67
  22   Hypotheses and probability 70
  23   Rhetorical questions and addressing your audience 73
  24   Comparing and contrasting 74
  25   Tying a text or presentation together 77
  26   Presenting results 80
  27   Interpreting findings 82

Contents

28	Concluding a study or presentation	85
29	Summary and abstract	89
30	Making a presentation	91
31	Writing academic emails	94

About the Concise PhraseBook

Science knows no country,
because knowledge belongs to humanity
Louis Pasteur

The Concise PhraseBook for Writing Academic English contains over 3000 phrases to help you write papers, reports, essays and theses at university and college.

The layout of the PhraseBook follows the structure of academic writing, including **Introduction, Method, Presenting Data, Literature Review, Arguing For and Against, Analysis, Presenting Results** and **Conclusions**. Additional sections include **Writing Academic Emails** and **Making a Presentation**.

The PhraseBook is suitable for university and college writing from Bachelor to Masters and PhD:

- Over 3000 phrases for academic writing
- Designed for native and non-native speakers
- Layout of the PhraseBook helps you structure your text
- Global English, including British and American spellings
- Exercises for individual and classroom use

Sections help you structure your text

The layout of the PhraseBook follows the structure of academic writing, giving you a framework to write in your subject and helping you structure your text. Below are some example phrases:

Introducing a study, chapter or section

The study will begin by outlining…
This study addresses a number of issues…
Chapters X and X concentrate on…
The following section sets out…
…to examine the research problem in detail
…to shed light on a number of problem areas in current theory
The paper presented here is based in part on an earlier study.

About the Concise PhraseBook

Defining the scope of your study

The focus of the study is...

The central question to be examined in this paper is...

The study is important for a number of reasons:

Present understanding of...is limited.

Previous studies have shown or suggested that...

The problem has been much discussed in recent literature.

This approach has a number of advantages: firstly,...

The present study was designed to test the hypothesis that...

Arguing for and against

This point is particularly relevant to...

This becomes clear when one examines...

This lends weight to the argument that...

Support for this interpretation comes from...

To put it another way,...

While it may well be valid that..., this study argues the importance of...

A serious drawback of this approach is...

One of the prime failings of this theory or explanation is...

Reviewing other work

X's work has had a profound influence on...

X takes little or no account of...

There is little evidence to suggest that...

The study offers only cursory examination of...

X gives a detailed if not always tenable analysis of...

The authors' claim that...is not well founded.

X's explanation is not implausible, if not entirely satisfactory.

Analysis and explanation

If, for the sake of argument, we assume...

One of the most obvious consequences of...is...

Although it may well be true that..., it is important not to overlook...

It is important to distinguish carefully between...

The extent to which this reflects...is unclear.

A more plausible explanation for or of...would...

The reason for...is unknown, but...has been suggested by X as a possible factor.

About the Concise PhraseBook

Summary and conclusions

Concluding this section, we can say that...
Chapter X draws together the main findings of the paper.
The study has gone some way towards understanding...
A number of key issues have been addressed in this study.
This study has highlighted a number of problem areas in existing theory.
While the initial findings are promising, further research is necessary.
The results of this study suggest a number of new avenues for research.

Vocabulary for university and college writing

Colloquial or slang expressions are usually avoided in academic writing: informally you may have a *hunch*, but in a paper or thesis you put forward a *hypothesis*. Sensing the distinction between formal and informal English can be difficult; however, all the phrases in the PhraseBook are in the correct style for university and college writing. The PhraseBook also includes many of the most frequent words in academic English, based on the *Academic Word List* by Averil Coxhead et al. of Victoria University of Wellington, New Zealand. These words are marked in italics.

Ellipsis dots ... mark where to insert your own words

The distinction between...and...
Based on..., we decided to...

X and Y mark where to insert a name

According to X, ...
Originally suggested by X, ... was subsequently developed further by Y

Alternatives are shown by *or* and *etc.*

The results show or demonstrate
The results show, demonstrate, indicate *etc.*

Optional words or phrases are in lighter text

This shows clearly that ...
X claims, in my view wrongly, that ...

British and US variants are shown by GB and US

X analyses GB or analyzes US ...
a vigorous defence GB or defense US of ...

About the Concise PhraseBook

Self-study or classroom teaching

The PhraseBook can be used both for self-study and in the classroom. In the classroom, we recommend that students start with a sample of their own writing, which they use as they work through the PhraseBook.

> **Students work on their own writing**
>
> Rather than working on texts that are irrelevant or uninteresting, students work on their own writing, helping them to improve their real work
>
> **Corpus of phrases, thematically grouped**
>
> The PhraseBook provides a corpus of phrases, thematically grouped, for use in teaching. Students work through the PhraseBook, expanding their text with phrases from each section. This helps students to think about the different parts of a text and how to structure their argument.
>
> **Writing exercises**
>
> Each section is followed by writing exercises

After working through the PhraseBook, students will have produced a better written, more polished text.

About the author

Stephen Howe, PhD, is a Professor at the Department of English and Graduate School of Humanities at Fukuoka University in Japan. He was originally a medical student, but gained his doctorate in Languages and Linguistics at the University of London.

He is an experienced editor of academic English and was cofounder of EnglishforResearch.com, an internet company specializing in academic editing, helping customers write, present and publish in English. Customers included faculty, students and researchers at over 430 universities, organizations and companies in more than 60 countries.

Stephen Howe has been a Visiting Fellow at Wolfson College, Cambridge University, a visiting academic at the University of Cape Town, and a Visiting Fellow at Macquarie University in Sydney. His research has been supported by the British Academy and the Japan Society for the Promotion of Science.

Also available

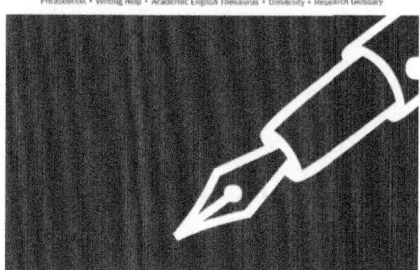

The Concise PhraseBook for Writing Academic English is based on the **PhraseBook for Writing Papers and Research in English**. The full PhraseBook contains about **5000 words and phrases**, plus **Writing Help**, an **Academic English Thesaurus** and a **Glossary of university and research terminology**.

The PhraseBook is used in **more than 30 countries worldwide** in subjects ranging from **Medicine, Engineering, Science** and **Technology** to **Law, Business** and **Economics, Political Science, Geography, History, Sociology, Psychology, Language** and **Education**.

What readers say about the PhraseBook

Here is what readers say about the PhraseBook for Writing Papers and Research in English:

★ ★ ★ ★ ★

Yes, yes, yes
A time saver for writing journal articles. It may also help when you don't know what to write next. (Amazon.com)

★ ★ ★ ★ ★

Easy to use
Love all the various suggestions on how to compose the same sentence. (Amazon.com)

■ Also available

★★★★★

Get this book!

Must have for students.

(Amazon.com)

★★★★★

Excellent and very helpful

Got this for my partner looking to write a PhD, she loved it. Has been really helpful to her.

(Amazon.co.uk)

★★★★★

Five Stars

Excellent book for consulting, well laid out, easy to follow and very complete.

(Amazon.co.uk)

★★★★★

Perfect for academia

This book really helped me write papers and literature reviews. Would recommend for anyone undertaking academic writing. (Amazon.co.uk)

★★★★★

Very useful book!

I'd been looking for a complete and simple phrasebook for a few days to help me writing my thesis. After a few attempts without being really convinced, I finally came across this book. It fits perfectly my needs and expectations. (Amazon.de)

★★★★★

Magic book for students

Very useful for my thesis!

(Amazon.de)

★★★★★

Sehr empfehlenswert

Das Buch ist sehr strukturiert aufgebaut. Man findet sich leicht zurecht und dementsprechend kann man gut damit arbeiten. Ich bin sehr zufrieden. (Amazon.de)

★★★★★

Good

Useful for research paper writing for all non native speakers of English and enhance the manuscript in all aspects of editing. (Amazon.in)

★★★★★

Utilissimo

Frasario utilissimo per trovare in breve tempo le migliori espressioni da utilizzare nella preparazione di un articolo o relazione di tipo scientifico. (Amazon.it)

Also available

Writing Help on style, spelling, punctuation and grammar

Writing Help sections give advice on Style, Spelling, Punctuation and Grammar, helping you avoid common errors.

Style

Varieties of English — Avoiding colloquial language — Avoiding contracted forms — Avoiding clichés — Avoiding tautology — Referring to yourself — Referring to the reader — Referring generally — *he* and *she* — Other types of bias

Spelling

British and US spellings — *z* and *s* spellings

Punctuation

Full stop or period — Comma — Semicolon — Colon — Question mark — Exclamation mark or point — Hyphen — Prefixes — The hyphen in fixed compounds — Using the hyphen in temporary compounds before a noun — Dash — The possessive with *'s* — Quotation marks — Punctuation at the end of quotations — Punctuating titles, legends and bullets — Parenthesis and ellipsis — References — Abbreviations — Capitalization

Grammar

Noncount nouns — Singular words ending in *-s* — Irregular plurals — Confusing words: singular and plural — Confusing words: pronouns — Irregular verbs

Academic English Thesaurus to expand your vocabulary

A thesaurus is a list of words with similar meanings. The PhraseBook thesaurus is specially compiled for university and research writing, and contains both synonyms (words with a similar meaning) and antonyms (words with the opposite meaning):

Key words for academic writing

It includes key words for academic writing, such as 'study', 'question', 'theory', 'prove'. These key words have simple umbrella headings, so that by looking up for example 'prove', you find alternatives such as *substantiate*, *establish*, *verify* and *corroborate*.

Antonyms

Antonyms, such as *disprove* or *fail to demonstrate*, are given in lighter text

Also available

The PhraseBook thesaurus helps you helps you write with a richer vocabulary, greater variety, and avoid using the same expressions over and again.

Glossary of university and research terminology

A great deal of English academic vocabulary derives from Latin and Greek; much has also been borrowed from or via French as well as from German, Italian and Arabic, for example, in psychology, music and mathematics. In addition, many of the abbreviations common in university and research writing – such as *e.g.*, *i.e.* and *etc.* – and many everyday academic terms – such as *campus*, *school* and *curriculum* – also derive from Latin or Greek.

As modern coinages such as *tele + vision* and *inter +* net show, Greek and Latin elements are still used to create new terms today. Knowledge of some Greek and Latin helps you to decipher the meaning of many words, not least for speakers from parts of the world with other classical languages. The PhraseBook includes:

Glossary of university and research terminology

Alma mater, curriculum vitae, extracurricular, magna cum laude, sophomore etc.

Glossary of Greek, Latin and other word elements

Astro, auto, bio, cracy, ecto, infra, nomy, ortho, para, syn, tele etc.

SI and British-American units

Feet, inches and yards, miles, pounds and ounces, gallons and pints etc.

PhraseBook	Full	Concise
Words and phrases	5000	3000
Writing Help	✓	—
Academic English Thesaurus	✓	—
Glossary	✓	—
Suitable for	University and research	University and college
ISBN	978 1 492959 79 3	978 1 903384 09 1

Phrases

1 Preface and acknowledgements

*Genius is two percent inspiration,
ninety-eight percent perspiration*
Thomas Edison

A preface is a short text at the beginning of a work. In it you thank – or *acknowledge* – people who have helped you. You can write a preface at the beginning of a thesis or dissertation, for example.

- The study was *conceived* as…
- When I began work on…, little did I realize…
- Needless to say, the faults remaining are entirely my own
- Of course, as is usual, all errors and oversights are entirely my own.

Thanks

- First of all, I would like to thank…
- First and foremost, I would like to thank…
- In particular, I would like to thank…
- I am especially grateful to…
- Many people have contributed either directly or indirectly to this study
- I would like to thank…
  - my *colleagues* at the Department of…at the University of…
  - my PhD supervisor at…University

- my late colleague,…
- my students at the University of…
- …for their helpful *comments*
- …for *comments* on an earlier *draft* of this manuscript or paper etc.
- …, who read an earlier *draft* of chapter…
- …, who kindly read through an earlier *version* of…
- …, who provided valuable or extensive *comments* on…
- …for her detailed *comments* on…
- …for help in the preparation of the manuscript or book
- …, who assisted in…
- …for *assistance* in or with…
- …for *technical assistance* in or with…
- …for his or her or their encouragement

Preface and acknowledgements

- …for his or her or their tireless enthusiasm
- …for his or her or their support
- …for granting me leave to write this book
- …for permission to use previously unpublished materials
- …for permission to reproduce figures
- I would like to thank my teacher or supervisor, X,
  - for awakening my interest in…
  - who encouraged me to…
  - who first introduced me to…
  - for a thorough grounding in the principles of…
- We have benefited greatly from the comments and suggestions of…
- I would also like to thank the reviewers of the previous edition for their constructive comments
- …the anonymous reviewers at…for their useful comments
- …is or are reprinted by kind permission of…
- I also wish to thank a number of people who…
- We would also like to thank…
- In addition, we would like to thank…
- I am also grateful to…
- Thanks are also due to X and Y
- Further thanks to…
- Thanks too to…
- …, and above all special thanks to…

Support, funding and approval

- We have benefited greatly from…
- We are indebted to…
- …for invaluable support
- I am deeply grateful for the assistance of…
- I would also like to acknowledge here my gratitude for…
- on behalf of all the co-authors
- I would like to thank…
  - …for their support of this research
  - …for the funding of this research
  - …for research grant 12345
  - …for funding of field work in…
- Financial support for this study was provided by…
- Partial support was provided by…
- This study was supported by the or a or an…Award for…
- The authors would like to acknowledge the financial support of…
- Grateful acknowledgement is made to…for grant number 12345
- …, which enabled me to…
  - carry out essential fieldwork
  - conduct interviews in…
  - purchase vital equipment for…
  - attend the conference on…in…
  - take a year's sabbatical
  - write up the final stages of my thesis
- The or this study was approved by the…Committee etc.
- a conflict of interest

Personal thanks

- Finally, I would like to add personal thanks to…
- Finally, I would like to thank…
- On a personal note,…
- And lastly,…

Preface and acknowledgements

- And most importantly,…
- …, without whom this would not have been possible
- …for her or his or their encouragement and support…
- …, when it seemed that this book or *thesis* would never be written
- To X
- For X
- To my husband or wife
- To my partner, X
- To my parents
- To my late father, X
- To my mother, X
- To my children, X and Y
- To my daughter, X
- To my son, X
- To my brother or sister, X, who…
- This book is dedicated to…
- …my wife or husband
- …my children
- …the memory of…, who…
- In memory of X

Writing practice 1: Preface and acknowledgements

1. Write a preface to your text using phrases from the section above

2. Write an acknowledgement thanking people who have helped you in your work

3. Using the words in italics in the section above, write five new phrases for your text

4. In class, in groups or in pairs, exchange texts and evaluate each other's writing, going through the points above

2 Writing a bio

Nothing in life is to be feared;
it is only to be understood
Marie Curie

A bio is a short biography of a scholar, author or speaker. It describes their academic career and achievements. You could write a bio for for a university or conference website or the jacket of a book, for example. You can also use the phrases to introduce a keynote or invited speaker before a talk.

Education and position

- X is Chair or Director of…
- X is Professor of…at the University of X
- X is the…Professor of…at…
- X is a lecturer GB in…at the University of X
- X is assistant professor US of…at the University of X
- X is a senior lecturer GB in…at the University of X
- X is associate professor US of…at the University of X
- Since 2024, she or he has taught…at…
- X has taught at…
- She has taught at various universities, including…
- X is a researcher in…at the…*Institute*
- X was a visiting professor, scholar etc. at…
- In 2024, X was a guest lecturer or a researcher at…
- X studied…at…with Professor A. Smith
- She received her PhD from the University of X in 2024
- He received his doctorate in…at…

- After graduating in…at…, X or he or she…
- She is currently…
- He was, until recently, Professor of…
- She was formerly…
- He was head of…between…and…
- She was head of…from…to…

Research and publications

- He is the *author* of…
- His *major* books include…
- Her most recent books are…
- Her publications include…
- Among her publications are…
- The *author* of papers on…, X…
- X is a leading *authority* on…
- X has *published* extensively in or on…
- X has *published* on various *aspects* of…
- Among her other books or publications are…
- His PhD examined…
- Her doctoral or master's *thesis* examined…
- He is a frequent contributor to…
- His main *research* interest is…

- Her *principal research* interests are...
- His *research* focuses on...
- His particular *area* of interest is...
- Her *research* interests include...
- She is currently editor of...
- X serves or has served on the editorial boards of...

Contributions and awards

- She was the...Award winner for her paper on...
- In 2024, X received the...Prize for...
- X has made a number of important contributions to...
- X was influential in establishing etc....
- X is widely *acknowledged* as...
- X is perhaps best known for his *research* on or *contribution* to...
- Her *contribution* to...is widely recognized
- In 2023, she was elected President, Chair etc. of...
- X is a member of the...Committee, Society etc....

Contributors

- X was responsible for...
  - the *design* of the study
  - *data* collection and *analysis*
- X contributed to the writing of the paper
- X assisted in writing the paper
- X supervised...
- X participated in...
- X provided important information on...
- X carried out a number of experiments
- X assisted in *data* collection and entry
- This study etc. was carried out in *partnership* with...

Writing practice 2: Writing a bio

1. Write a bio about yourself using the phrases above
2. Write a bio about someone in your class
3. Using the words in italics in the section above, write five new phrases for your bio
4. In class, in groups or in pairs, exchange texts and evaluate each other's writing, going through the points above

3 Introducing a study or presentation

All truths are easy to understand, once they are discovered;
the point is, to discover them
Galileo Galilei

The phrases in this section help you introduce your work. Use the phrases under 'Structure' to describe how your paper or presentation is organized. This will help your reader or audience picture your text or talk in their mind. Use headings to clearly signpost the main sections of your paper or presentation. Clear headings and good structure are like a road map, enabling your reader or audience to navigate your text smoothly.

- This *volume* is…
- This study investigates…
- This paper examines…
- This collection of papers presents…
- This special issue…
- The present *volume* contains…
- This paper puts forward…
- This paper will show…
- The study includes chapters on…
- This *chapter* presents…
- a presentation of…
- The question to be asked here is…
- The question to be examined in this paper is…
- In broad outline,…
- An *obvious* starting point is…
- …is generally taken as a or the starting point in discussing etc.…
- Before embarking on a discussion of…, it is important to…

Structure

- The study is divided into two etc. or several parts
- The study is divided into four etc. main sections
- The first *chapter*…; the second *chapter*…; the *final chapter*…
- The first two etc. chapters examine…
- *Chapter* X discusses…
- *Chapter* X addresses a number of *issues*…
- Chapters X–X concentrate on…
- Firstly, secondly, thirdly…
- Firstly,…, followed by…, and finally…
- In part 1,…; in part 2,…; and in part 3…
- The central *theme* is…
- The question to be asked here is…
- the subject of inquiry
- to examine the *research* problem in detail
- By way of introduction,…
- the study will begin by outlining or examining…
- it seems *appropriate* to…
- …give a *brief* overview of the problem
- …provide a *brief* outline of…
- …outline the *investigation*
- It will highlight…
- The following *section* sets out…

Introducing a study or presentation

- This *section* will examine…
- …is or are introduced in this *section* or *chapter*
- The *analysis* in *chapter* X…
- In X.X it is argued that…
- In X.X the importance of…as a factor…is discussed
- This is followed by…

Related work

- The paper presented here is based *in part* on an earlier study
- An earlier *version* of this paper was presented at…
- …was published in the *Journal* of…
- This paper…
- …is a revised *version* of…
- …has been substantially revised
- …includes new chapters on…
- There are new sections on…
- This paper etc. forms part of a larger study of…
- This paper etc. has been *submitted* for publication in…
- Parts of this study have been or were presented at the *conference* on…
- Parts of this paper were presented in a *lecture* on…to…in April 2024 etc.

Writing practice 3: Introducing a study or presentation

1. Using phrases from the section above, write an introduction to your text or presentation
2. Using the words in italics in the section above, write five new phrases for your text or presentation
3. In class, in groups or in pairs, evaluate each other's writing or presentations, going through the points above

19

4 The aim of your study and outlining the topic

Although I cannot move and I have to speak through a computer
in my mind I am free
Stephen Hawking

The phrases in this section help you state the aim of your study and outline your topic. You can also discuss what is already known about your topic and why your study is important.

- The study examines…
- This study investigates…
- The study addresses…
- This study puts forward…
- The study will attempt to show…
- This study seeks to explain…
- This study attempts to clarify…
- This study evaluates…
- The study seeks to combine…
- The study seeks to integrate…
- *integration* of…and…
- The study aims to…
- The purpose of this study is to…
- The purpose of the present paper is to…
- The study focuses on…
- It will highlight…
- …to explore…
- …to examine…
- …to explain…
- …to attempt to…
- …to develop…
- …to determine whether…
- …to define…
- …to account for…
- …to identify…
- …to replicate…
- the *concept* of…
- the question whether…
- the first question is whether…
- a or one key question relates to…
- the *fundamental* questions concerning…
- the issue of…
- the problem of…
- the problem of how to…
- the need to…
- the origin of…
- the effect of…on…
- the possible effects of…on…
- the relationship between…and…
- Our main aim or *objective* here is to…
- the *overall* aim or *objective* of…
- a general explanation for…
- We will show how…
- We will show that…
- What we aim to *achieve* is…
- …, with the aim of establishing a *framework*…
- …in the *framework* of a general *theory* of…
- The aim of this study is twofold, threefold etc.:
- The aim or *objective* of the study is…
- …to put forward an explanation for…
- …to put forward a *theory* of or for…
- …to examine the types of…
- …to verify the *role* of…in…

The aim of your study and outlining the topic

- ...to investigate what *role*, if any,...plays in...
- ...to assess the effects of...on...
- ...to *trace* the development of...
- ...to improve the or our understanding of...
- ...to broaden our understanding of...
- ...to gain new *insights* into...
- ...to provide better insight into...
- ...to highlight a number of...
- ...to direct attention towards...
- ...to establish a theoretical *framework*...
- ...to find a *unified* basis for...
- ...to lay the foundations of or for...
- ...to introduce new terminology
- ...to make recommendations for...
- ...to address the *issues* of...
- ...to move beyond...
- ...to identify and evaluate...
- ...to evaluate or examine critically...
- ...to evaluate empirically...
- ...to examine the value of...
- ...to examine the *validity* of...
- ...to examine the nature of...
- ...to determine the relationship between...
- ...to examine the development of...
- ...to examine the effects of...on...
- ...to examine whether...is affected by...
- ...to examine to what extent...is affected by...
- ...to elaborate on the idea that or of...
- ...to stimulate the *debate* on...
- Our contention is that...
- The present study was designed to test the *hypothesis* that...
- a combination of breadth of coverage and depth of detail

- This study seeks to strike a balance between...and...

Current understanding

- to re-examine...
- to revisit...
- ...the long-standing issue of...
- ...the long-standing question
- to take up and build on earlier *research*
- The issue, problem, cause etc. of...
- ...merits further study
- ...deserves further consideration
- ...is worth examining more closely
- ...is worth exploring further
- ...has not yet been addressed fully
- ...is neglected in current *theory*
- ...is not yet clearly understood
- ...is not yet completely understood
- ...is not well understood
- ...is poorly understood
- *successive* attempts have failed to solve
- this *approach* gives a better basis for...
- The problem is a *complex* one.
- ...presents a difficult set of problems
- ...poses a number of problems:
- ...poses particular problems in cases where...
- the prevailing view is that...
- ...is widely *perceived* as...
- the question has been raised whether...
- Present understanding of...is limited.
- the field of...is still relatively undeveloped
- there is as yet or at present no consensus on...
- As yet, no one explanation has gained acceptance.

The aim of your study and outlining the topic

- there is at present little agreement on the causes of etc....
- there is at present no general agreement on the causes of etc....
- there is still *considerable* disagreement on the causes of etc....
- the *mechanism* by which...is unknown or not well understood
- the controversial question of...
- much of our knowledge of...comes from...
- the *task* of...is complicated further by...
- The *impact* of...on...is not easy to determine
- The effect of...on...has not been examined in detail.
- its effects on...have not previously been studied in *detail*

Importance of the study

- The study is important for a number of reasons:
- The study is of relevance because...
- It is important to...
- the importance of...

- an important aspect of...
- ...is an important or urgent subject for study
- ...is needed
- ...is necessary
- ...warrants further *investigation*
- ...warrants closer scrutiny or examination
- The problem merits further *investigation*.
- ...is worth examining for its own sake
- ...to shed light on a number of *issues* or problem areas in current *theory*
- *Resolution* of this problem would...
- the *prospect* of a breakthrough in...
- Other authors have also called for...
- This study, *thesis*, paper etc.
- ...may show or reveal...
- ...may stimulate the *debate* on...
- ...may provide *evidence* of or for...
- ...may contribute to our understanding of...
- ...may contribute towards a better understanding of...
- ...may offer an *alternative* view or explanation of...
- ...may *enable* a better explanation of...

Writing practice 4: The aim of your study and outlining the topic

1. Using some of the phrases above, write a section on the aim of your study and outline your study topic

2. Write and present a poster on your work, either individually or in groups or pairs

3. Using the words in italics in the section above, write five new phrases for your text

4. In class, in groups or in pairs, exchange texts and evaluate each other's writing, going through the points above

5 Defining the scope of your study or presentation

I know nothing except the fact of my ignorance
Socrates

Scope means the range or extent of your study. Use the phrases in this section to explain what you will include in your study or presentation, and what you will exclude. This is important to give your text or talk a clear outline or frame.

- The *focus* of the study is…
- The study focuses on…
- The inquiry focused on…
- The study encompasses…
- The study incorporates…
- The question to be asked here is…
- The central question to be examined in this paper *etc.* is…
- …is or are central to this study
- …is or are discussed in detail
- More specifically,…
- a or one condition *imposed* by…is…
- What we are mainly concerned with here…
- a *focus* on…
- an *emphasis* on…
- in the *context* of…
- to seek *initial* answers to…
- to provide a basis for…
- …will be expanded upon
- a simplified *approach* to…
- an *empirical approach*
- a more theoretical *approach* to…
- a purely theoretical *approach*

What is excluded from study

- The aim or purpose of this study is not to…
- …is or are not central to this study
- …is or are not discussed in detail
- …is beyond the *scope* of this study
- …falls outside this study
- …, which can only be discussed briefly here
- …, only some of which can be discussed here
- It excludes…
- …is distinct from…
- …was *excluded* from the study
- While it would be interesting to examine…in greater detail,…
- we have decided here to…
- we have purposely *excluded*…
- *access* to…is difficult
- one problem *inherent* in…is…
- For the purpose of this study, paper *etc.*, we will confine the discussion to…
- our *priority* here is to…
- attention will be *restricted* here to…
- I have *restricted* myself to…

Defining the scope of your study or presentation

- the or my intention is not to…
- It is not the *task* of this study to…
- We make no claims here of or that…
- I do not wish to imply by this study that…

Further references

- A fuller discussion of…will appear in a later *publication*.
- …will be taken up in a later *publication*
- …see X (*forthcoming*)
- …see X (in press)

- references are given at the end of the paper
- for further discussion see for *example*…
- …is discussed in detail by or in X
- see X for complete *data*
- see X for a *summary* and references
- For a *survey* or review of…, see X
- For an in-depth review of…, see X
- For further information on…, see X
- For a more detailed examination of…, see X
- For a bibliography of studies on…, see X

Writing practice 5: Defining the scope of your study or presentation

1. Using phrases from the section above, outline the scope of your study or presentation

a. Also discuss what is excluded from your study or presentation

2. Using the words in italics in the section above, write five new phrases for your text

3. In class, in groups or in pairs, exchange texts and evaluate each other's writing, going through the points above

6 Your method or approach

The scientist is not a person who gives the right answers,
[s]he is one who asks the right questions
Claude Lévi-Strauss

Use the phrases in this section to explain your method or approach. Here you can discuss the type of study you will make, your methods, and the reasons for your approach.

Type of study

- an *initial* study of…
- an exploratory study of…
- a pilot study of…
- an overview of…
- a *survey* of…
- a critical *survey* of…
- a *comprehensive investigation* of…
- a detailed *analysis* of…
- an in-depth *analysis* of…
- a comparative study of…
- a comparative *investigation* of…
- a comparison of…
- a theoretical *approach*
- a theoretical *analysis* of…
- a statistical *analysis* of…
- an *empirical* study or *investigation* of…
- a *series* of experiments
- to *conduct* an experiment on…
- a field study of…
- a case study of…
- a chronological account of…
- a programme GB or program US to or of…
- a questionnaire completed by…
- interviews carried out between…and…at or in…

- a new *approach*
- a new *approach* to the problem of…
- a holistic *approach*

Method

- by examining…
- …is or can be *obtained* by…
- with the help of…
- with the *aid* of…
- by means of…
- by application of…
- A useful tool for…is…
- an indispensable tool in…
- this *device* enables us to…
- we have a number of techniques at our *disposal*
- …, drawing on…
- incorporating a number of…
- in the *context* of…
- in conjunction with…
- based primarily on…
- a *process* involving…
- within the *framework* of…
- a or the frame of reference
- First we *select*…; we then *select*…

Your method or approach

- Stage or step 1 involves…. In stage or step 2, we…
- *Phase* 1…; *phase* 2…; *phase* 3…
- We used…
- …to study the effects of…on…
- …to examine the effects of…on…
- …to model the effects of…on…
- …to *estimate* the effects of…on…
- To determine whether…, we…
- To assess whether…, we…
- To measure the effects of…on…, we…
- To assess whether…was affected by…, we…
- To investigate whether…, we analysed GB or analyzed US…
- …was or were measured by…
- …was determined for each…by…
- …was measured before and after…
- …was used to measure…
- …was equipped with…
- …was transferred to…
- …was or is used in the *analysis* of…to determine…
- …provides a useful *estimate* of or for…
- the *simulation* showed that…
- in the presence of…
- in the absence of…
- after addition of…
- *substitution* of…for…
- if the constraints are *relaxed*
- measurements were made or taken at…sites
- background measurements, samples etc. were taken…
- …under these conditions…
- …following the *method* outlined in…
- …according to standard *criteria*
- …following standard *procedure*
- …in accordance with standard procedures
- …was performed according to a or the standard…*protocol*
- …following the manufacturer's *guidelines* or *instructions*
- …according to the manufacturer's *guidelines* or *instructions*
- …as *specified* in the manufacturer's *guidelines* or *instructions*
- For this we can use a number of *strategies*
- One *option* here would be to…
- *Adjustment* of…allows us to…
- …is *enhanced* if we…
- This *method* can be used to obtain…
- This *technology* enables us to…
- The most usual *method* is…
- …is commonly used in…to measure etc.…
- …by the…*method*
- …according to the…*method*
- …as previously described by X
- …using the…procedures described by X et al.
- …using the…*method* as *modified* by X
- …later *modified* by X
- …adapted from X et al.
- our *adaptation* of the…or X's method
- X and Y *advocate* the use of…
- The *method* etc. can also be adapted or extended to…
- Using this *method* or technique, we are or were able to…

Reasoning

- to verify…
- to establish…
- to *facilitate*…
- to *capture*…
- to measure accurately…
- the reason for this is…
- Because of this,…
- it should be stressed that…
- we might expect that…
- it is convenient to…
- it is helpful to consider…
- It is helpful here to…
- In practice,…
- the application of…to…
- Particular attention will be paid to…
- to examine more closely
- …will be or was investigated further by…
- …will be examined in greater detail
- Based on…, we decided to…
- This has been shown to…
- In doing so,…
- it will be useful to examine…
- …deserves special attention
- we opted to…
- from this *perspective*
- This *approach* is based on…
- …is frequently used to…
- The experiment was designed to…
- *Previous* measurements based on…have shown that…
- The *traditional* approach has been to…
- This *innovation* allows us to…
- The most *straightforward* way of…is…
- This *route* would enable us to…
- This is the course or *method* adopted here.
- The advantage of this *approach* is that…
- This *approach* has the advantage of or that…
- This *approach* has a number of advantages: firstly,…
- …gives a better basis for…
- it combines…with or and…
- This *format* allows us to see more clearly how…
- In this way, we are or were able to *target*…
- This enables one to *create*…
- …allows or enables the *transfer* of…from…to…
- such a *rigid* approach does not allow…
- this approach gives greater *flexibility*
- this *construction* allows us to…
- This rather strict *regime* ensures that…
- By *monitoring*…, we are or were able to…
- This allows…to be examined within the same *framework*.
- In this way, we are able to *eliminate* several of the problems of previous *approaches* or methods
- One difficulty in…is…
- A or one *significant* problem is…
- *Coordination* of…and…is essential or particularly difficult
- a compromise
- One strategy would be to…
- …avoids this difficulty by…
- the practical problems *involved* in…
- an *alternative* way of approaching the problem
- Another way of looking at the question of…
- If, however, we reformulate the question, we…

Your method or approach

- It is impossible to discuss, examine etc....without discussing...
- It is impossible to discuss, examine etc....without reference to...
- ...methodological *issues*...
- The original or earlier *method* was abandoned because of problems with...
- Conventional methods, *techniques* etc. are unable to...
- ...cannot be achieved by conventional methods

Controls

- In control experiments, we found that...
- under control conditions
- under *similar* conditions
- ...in a temperature-controlled *environment*

- The experiment was carried out at room temperature.
- To control..., we...
- To control the effects of..., it is necessary to...
- ...serves as an important check on...
- ...in order to avoid...
- ...to prevent...
- ...to correct for...
- ...may be corrected by...
- To *ensure* that..., we...
- ...can be ensured by...
- It is relatively easy to control for or check that...
- We went to great lengths to *ensure*...
- this is or can be *minimized* by...
- It is particularly important to...
- It is important to bear in mind...

Writing practice 6: Your method or approach

1. Using phrases from the section above, outline your method or approach. Discuss

a. Your method

b. Why you chose your method or approach

c. Any materials and controls

2. Using the words in italics in the section above, write five new phrases for your text

3. In class, in groups or in pairs, exchange texts and evaluate each other's writing, going through the points above

7 Definitions, notation and terminology

*In my view, all that is necessary for faith is the belief that
by doing our best we shall succeed in our aims: the improvement of mankind*
Rosalind Franklin

The phrases in this section help you define any special terms in your study: what they mean and how you will use them.

- the types of…
- in terms of…
- with reference to…
- this *formula* allows us to…
- We defined…as…
- By…we mean…
- By…is meant…
- …is defined as…
- …can be defined as…
- …is or are often defined as…
- …are defined in this study as follows:
- …can be characterized as…
- …can be formulated as follows:
- …denotes…
- …represents
- …is representative of…
- …, which is or are represented here by or as…
- …can be written as…
- …are classified as…
- …can be classified as either…or…
- …can be classified by…into two, several etc. *categories*
- …can be categorized as…
- …can be *specified* as follows:
- …can be grouped into a number of different types:
- …derives from…

- …is *derived* from…
- …are labelled GB or labeled US as…
- we can *label* this…
- …can perhaps be termed…
- …satisfies the *definition* of…as…
- …accounts for…
- …are exclusively…
- …is primarily…
- …should essentially be viewed as…

Rules and laws

- as a rule
- a general rule
- a rule of thumb
- the rules that govern…
- according to X's Law
- …is said to be…when or if…
- If…, then…is said to be…
- in *principle*
- a basic tenet of…
- …is based on the *principle* of…
- according to the *guidelines* laid down by…
- an important or a *fundamental principle* that underlies…
- *violation* of this principle results in or would mean that…

Definitions, notation and terminology

Use and reference

- in the sense of or that…
- in the *context* of…
- in effect
- de facto
- The terms…are used as…
- in the sense described or discussed above
- In this study, the term…refers to…
- In this paper, the term…will be used to refer to…
- In this study,…designates…
- In its strictest sense, the term… denotes…
- a narrow *definition* of…
- The term…is used here in a *somewhat restricted* sense
- This can be expressed in terms of…
- …can be expressed as follows:
- …is taken here to include…
- …of a given type
- …also falls into this category
- …may well also fall into this category
- …known collectively as…
- in more general terms
- Broadly speaking,…
- In its most general sense,…refers to…
- …is used here as an umbrella term
- This enables various types of…to be grouped under one heading.
- …can be subsumed under the heading…
- This *definition* can also be applied to…
- The *definition* of…overlaps with…
- to extend the *definition* of…to include…
- If…is viewed or defined as…, then…
- this *definition* allows us to speak of…
- …is used as a convenient shorthand for…

- a convenient abbreviation for or of…
- in other words
- Other possible terms are…
- An *alternative definition* of or for…is…
- An *alternative* way of representing…is…
- …is another way of saying…
- in lay terms
- to use a term loosely
- for want of a better term
- This can be labelled GB or labeled US, for want of a better term, as…
- This *definition* hinges on…

Following others' definitions

- In this study,…is used as in X
- X terms this…
- X labels this…
- …, as defined by X
- …can be classified, according to or using X's terminology, as…
- various notations are used in the literature
- …, a term coined by X
- The term…was coined by X to *denote* or describe…
- …was first used by X to describe etc.…
- The first use of…was…
- The *concept* of…was introduced by X to…
- The *notion* of…derives from…
- This *principle* etc. is known as…after X
- …is named after X, who…
- …adopted from X
- …largely or to some extent borrowed from X
- It seems best, following X, to…

Definitions, notation and terminology

- X recognizes two etc. types of…, which she or he terms…
- various definitions have been suggested in the literature
- a widely accepted *definition*
- …is usually accepted as…
- For the sake of clarity, we have *retained* X's nomenclature…
- The term…is commonly or often or sometimes used to refer to…
- …is conventionally labelled GB or labeled US…
- …can be labelled GB or labeled US…according to the *convention*…
- For this reason…is often labelled GB or labeled US…
- Most usually…refers to…
- Usually,…is labelled GB or labeled US…
- it is customary to speak of…
- what has come to be known as…
- …is or are also known as…
- …(also known as…)
- …variously termed…
- the terms…and…are sometimes, often etc. used interchangeably
- Some writers etc. use the terms…and…interchangeably
- …later *modified* by X
- X uses…in a *somewhat restricted* sense
- The term…originally referred to…; however, it is now used…
- For historical reasons,…is often labelled GB or labeled US…
- …are traditionally categorized as…
- …are traditionally divided into a number of *categories* or groups etc.…
- the *so-called*…
- This *definition* differs to some extent from…

Exceptions

- Unless stated otherwise,…
- …unless indicated otherwise
- apart from the…noted or discussed above
- The term is not used here in the sense of…
- The term is not used here in the conventional sense
- The term…is taken from X, but is here used differently: in this study it refers to or is defined as…

Writing practice 7: Definitions, notation and terminology

1. Using phrases from the section above, discuss the definitions, notation and terminology in your text
   a. Define any terms you use
   b. Discuss where you have followed others' definitions
2. Using the words in italics in the section above, write five new phrases for your text
3. In class, in groups or in pairs, exchange texts and evaluate each other's writing, going through the points above

8 Presenting data

An experiment is a question which science poses to Nature, and a measurement is the recording of Nature's answer
Max Planck

Use the phrases below to present your data. You can also describe any figures, tables and graphs.

- …can be expressed more simply as…
- …is or was determined as follows:
- …is or was measured by…
- …is or was calculated as follows:
- …is or was calculated by…
- where…
  - is the…
  - represents
  - denotes
- only half of…
- over half of…
- the *ratio* of…to…
- expressed as a percentage of…
- The *proportion* of…ranged from…to…
- ranging from…to…
- …ranked in order of…
- …is proportional to…
- …was significantly higher in…than in…
- …was significantly lower in…
- …peaked at…
- …was higher than expected
- …was lower than expected
- the expected number of…
- *items* 1 to 5 show…
- For the sake of *clarity* or brevity, we have omitted…
- *supplementary* data can be obtained from the authors

Figures, tables and graphs

- table X shows…
- figure X illustrates…
- as seen in figure X
- as shown in the table above or below
- examples of…are shown in figure or table X
- The *image* shows that…
- The figures, *data* etc.…
- …are given above
- …are presented below
- …are shown in table X
- …are listed above or below
- …are summarized in figure or table X
- …are *illustrated* in figure X
- …are *illustrated* in the figure, graph or table above or below
- …are shown in the graph above or below
- …are shown in brackets or parentheses
- …are given in the *appendix*
- Figure X shows…
- …the size of…
- …the level of…
- …the extent of…
- …the effect of…
- …the rate of…
- …the *concentration* of…

Presenting data

- …the *distribution* of…
- All values are given as…
- each column represents…
- The shaded *area* represents…
- …is shown superimposed on…
- …based on the *data* given in table etc. X
- Values in brackets or parentheses are…
- An *alternative* way of presenting…is to…

Describing figures and graphs

- a rise
- an increase
- a sharp rise or increase in…
- a steady rise or increase in…
- a gradual increase
- an *initial* rise followed by a steady etc. decrease
- …peaked at…
- a peak of…
- a decrease
- a fall
- a sharp *decline* or decrease or fall in…
- a drop of … *percent*
- a reduction in…
- a steady decrease in…
- shows an upward or a downward *trend*
- …remained *constant*
- marked as a shaded *area* in figure X
- shown by a solid line
- marked by a dotted line
- the top left of the figure
- the top right of the table
- in the centre GB or center US or middle of the graph
- centre GB or center US right or left
- the bottom left of the graph
- the bottom right of the figure

Data sources and collection

- *primary* sources were:
- secondary sources included…
- an extensive database
- to collect *data* on…
- We *obtained data* on…from…
- *Data* on…were collected…
- …by…
- …between…and…
- …during…
- …at regular intervals…
- …continuously
- The data were or are *compiled* from a number of or several sources
- the *bulk* of the data was collected…
- Continuous measurements of…were made…
- Sampling of…was carried out over a two-week etc. *period* in July 2024.
- Conditions during the sampling *period* were…
- a *random* sample of…
- …selected or chosen at *random* from…
- …randomly selected from…
- …provides a representative sample of…
- It is estimated that there are…
- No *data* were *available* for or on…
- …is or are omitted here for the sake of brevity
- (*data* not shown)
- It is the university's *policy* to…
- All participants gave their informed *consent*
- Participation in the study was *voluntary*
- We would like to thank…for their *participation* in the study.

33

■ **Giving examples**

> **Writing practice 8: Presenting data**
>
> 1. Using phrases from the section above, discuss the data used in your text or talk
> a. Add a figure, table or graph and label it
> b. Outline your data sources and method of collection
>
> 2. Using the words in italics in the section above, write five new phrases for your text or talk
>
> 3. In class, in groups or in pairs, evaluate each other's writing or presentations, going through the points above

9 Giving examples

Simplicity is the ultimate sophistication
Leonardo da Vinci

In academic writing it is important to give examples and cite evidence to support your argument. The phrases in this section help you do that.

- for example…
- e.g.
- such as…
- for *instance*…
- compare…
- To illustrate:
- this is *illustrated* by…
- …, as…illustrates
- as in the following *equation*
- Take, for example, the case of…
- As a case in point, consider…
- note for example…
- in each case
- one example of…is…
- one such case…
- one example concerns…

- one *instance*…
- one example as illustration…
- To mention or cite one example:…
- as seen in the following *quotation* by X
- In this example,…
- compare similarly…
- a striking example of…is…
- a classic example of…is…
- a classic case of…
- a clear-cut case of…
- a graphic illustration of…
- To take a concrete example:…
- a number of *specific* examples are given later in the paper
- a more recent example
- a typical example of…

Giving examples

- an oft-quoted example
- a frequently *cited* example of…
- Examples of…are…
- Instances of…*occur* or are found in…
- a number of examples of…are given below
- examples of…were given above
- in the footnote below
- in note X
- see footnotes X and Y
- examples are listed or given in the *appendix*
- …are given in the bibliography
- There are numerous examples of…
- *plus* a number of other…
- Examples abound of…
- …, only some of which can be discussed here
- To take the most striking example,…
- Other notable examples are…
- A further example of…is…
- Further examples of…are…
- It is *very* difficult to cite an example or a single case of…

What the examples show

- The examples show…
- This example shows…
- The example demonstrates…
- These examples *indicate*…
- What these examples clearly illustrate is that…
- This serves to illustrate…
- …provides strong *empirical evidence* of or for…
- each point is *illustrated* with examples
- The case of…illustrates how or why…

- The case or example is instructive because or as it provides…
- as the examples below show or *demonstrate*
- as is evident from…
- the example of…has often been *cited* as…
- As an illustration, compare the following examples
- *evidence* from actual studies of…shows…
- *evidence* also exists that…
- in a recent etc. *survey* of…
- There may be further *evidence* for…
- The examples suggest…
- What is the *empirical* basis or *evidence* for…?
- …(unpublished *data*)
- anecdotal *evidence*
- the *evidence* for…is purely anecdotal
- This clearly illustrates the problem of…
- a counterexample to…
- There are no examples of…

Interviews

- In interviews, respondents stated that…
- Typical responses were…
- Typical statements were…
- Typical *comments* by interviewees were…
- …, as mentioned by several respondents
- The following quote illustrates…
- As one interviewee stated,…
- X states, for example, that…
- This was expressed by one respondent as…

■ **Literature review and the relationship to other work**

> **Writing practice 9: Giving examples**
>
> 1. Using phrases from the section above, add some examples to your text or presentation
> a. Discuss what the examples show
>
> 2. Using the words in italics in the section above, write five new phrases for your text or talk
>
> 3. In class, in groups or in pairs, evaluate each other's writing or presentations, going through the points above

10 Literature review and the relationship to other work

> *Ignorance more frequently begets confidence than does knowledge:*
> *it is those who know little, not those who know much,*
> *who so positively assert that this or that problem will never be solved by science*
> Charles Darwin

In a literature review, you survey what has been already written on your topic. *Literature* here does not mean Shakespeare or Jane Austen, rather previous research. You evaluate previous research and explain how and where your study fits in. You may also be able to identify any gaps in the literature – which you can then try to fill.

- As is well known,…
- It is well known that…
- …widely accepted…
- Many authors agree that…
- …broadly agree that…
- Many or most authors would agree that…
- a widely held belief
- a widely accepted *notion*
- our present understanding of…
- a common theoretical position
- the most widely accepted explanation of…is that…
- the prevailing view of…is that…

- the current consensus is that…
- Most or many or some scholars view…as…
- Most authors would interpret this as…
- …is usually interpreted as…
- …is generally analysed GB or analyzed US as…
- …is generally regarded as…
- within…*theory*
- from a…*perspective*
- within the *framework* of…
- a or the frame of reference

Literature review and the relationship to other work

Previous work

- As in *previous* studies of…,…
- …, as put forward in the study of…by X
- …originally proposed by X
- …first shown or demonstrated by X
- …in the writing of X
- …can be traced to…
- in his or her earlier work
- in her or his 2024 doctoral *thesis*
- initial *reaction* to X's paper was mixed
- The *notion* of…derives from…
- …has or have been the subject or the *focus* of numerous studies
- …has or have been discussed, examined etc. extensively in the literature
- several or various explanations etc. have been suggested in the literature
- a great many explanations etc. have been put forward for…
- The *topic* is not a new one; however,…
- There is now a substantial body of *research* or literature or work on…
- the wealth of literature on…
- Noteworthy studies of…are…
- X's most influential work
- X and Y, in their influential study of…,…
- …has been carried out in detail by X
- The most detailed examination or study of…to date is…
- *Initial* observations suggest or *indicate* that…
- *Previous* studies of or on…have shown or suggested that…
- Results from earlier studies have indicated or suggested that…
- *Research* conducted in the 1990s etc. indicated that…
- this has led some authors to suggest that…
- It has been shown or demonstrated repeatedly that…
- This view can be found in…
- a number of other studies…
- In a *preliminary* or an exploratory study, X found that…
- …has been linked to…
- …, which is also known to cause etc.…
- …has been found to have an adverse effect on…
- …has been shown to play an important or a pivotal *role* in…
- X first remarked on the similarity, relationship or connection between…
- Originally suggested by X in 1990 etc.,…was subsequently developed further by Y
- X's discovery of…
- …paved the way for…
- …was taken up by others…
- …provided the impetus for further *research* on etc.…
- …was the *trigger* for an explosion of research on…
- …contributed to the development of…
- …marked a *major* turning point in…
- X showed that…
- X and Y's study was the first to show etc. that or how…
- …was the first *major* work in or on…
- Before X, it was widely believed that…
- X's work, little recognized at the time, has come to be regarded as…
- though not *published* in his or her lifetime
- …now widely used in…
- X's study or work *established*…

Literature review and the relationship to other work

- X's study laid the groundwork for…
- the or a cornerstone of…*theory*
- the *foundation* of…*theory*
- Of *fundamental* importance to…is…
- The most detailed or *explicit* statement of…*theory* is…
- Building on or drawing on X's work,…
- X's *theory* is obviously of relevance or applicable here
- The…presented here is based in part on an earlier study
- Many of our or the findings confirm…found by X
- Based on these results,…
- Against this backdrop,…
- In view of this, it is useful to…
- Taking this on board, we can state that…
- Interestingly, some studies show…
- A number of investigators have shown…
- Some studies have reported…, while others have shown…
- Several authors or researchers have commented on…
- Previously, it was widely assumed that…
- Until recently, it was widely believed that…
- Many scholars adhere to the view that…
- Historically,…
- Traditionally,…
- Conventionally,…
- …is or was often *attributed* to…
- …is or was largely *attributed* to…
- We now know that…

Current work

- a topical *area* of *research*
- *issues* currently under discussion
- …has recently gained currency
- an *area* that has become increasingly important
- An increasing amount of literature is *devoted* to…
- This is reflected in current *research* on…
- …has or have been debated widely in the *media*
- research *undertaken* by X and Y in the last ten etc. years has shown that…
- *Attitudes* to…vary from…to…
- Recent work or *research* suggests that…
- X and Y have proposed that…
- A number of commentators have suggested that…
- Recently, it has been suggested or demonstrated that…
- It has recently been shown that…
- a new and interesting observation
- A comparatively recent study on or of…is…
- …presented recently…
- …is the subject of work in progress
- Recent *research* on…has made great strides towards…
- Recently, there have been important advances in…
- The last few years have witnessed…
- …a *shift* towards…
- …an increase in…
- …a surge of interest in…
- …renewed interest in…
- …a revival of…
- the *ongoing* effort to…
- …*complement* current or existing *research*
- The problem has been much discussed in recent literature.

- ...has attracted *considerable* or *widespread* interest...
- *Similar* results have been found in..., suggesting that...
- ...is *similar* to that reported by X
- ...is *similar* to results recently *published* by X
- ...parallels X's findings
- ...has *emerged* as the most likely explanation for...
- This *interpretation* or explanation is supported by earlier work on...by X
- Their work has yielded a number of promising new avenues of *research*
- ...has prompted new ways of looking at...
- Another possibility considered in *previous* studies is that...
- A growing number of researchers share the view of...as...
- This is often taken to support the view that...
- This is based on the belief that...
- a long-standing question
- the long-standing issue of...
- ...are known to exist
- a new line of inquiry

Contrasting work

- Another view is that...
- ..., *whereas* X believes that...
- a competing *theory*
- This contrasts with...who found that...
- In *contrast*, a study of...found or reported or showed...
- this *interpretation* has recently been challenged, however
- X's *theory*, explanation etc. has been challenged on various or several grounds:
- Although *research* suggests that..., *previous* studies have...
- Although early work or results suggested that..., *subsequent* studies have shown...
- Current *theory*, as it stands, does not adequately account for...
- A number of *aspects* of the problem require further *investigation*.
- Although a number of studies exist on...,
- ...still a great deal of disagreement
- ...has been hotly debated in the literature
- a bone of contention
- a *source* or hotbed of *controversy*
- *Controversy* remains regarding...
- Although controversial,...
- critics of...*theory* would argue that...
- X and Y's *response* is that...
- X's views have failed to gain *widespread* acceptance
- X has been criticized for failing to take account of etc....
- We *rejected* X's hypothesis on the basis of or that...
- This is reflected in X's findings that...
- Previous studies have *ignored*...
- The question has been raised whether...
- There are increasing doubts about...
- Many scholars doubt, however, whether or that...
- Other authors have also called for...
- Many authors have stressed the importance of...
- Few authors would dispute that...
- A number of other studies have argued or suggested that...

Literature review and the relationship to other work

- The *traditional* approach has been to…
- An *alternative*…, suggested by X, is…
- However, recent *research* by X…suggests that…
- X and Y have also pointed out *or* to…
- Researchers have traditionally been *reluctant* to…
- Researchers adopting this position include for example…
- …is beginning to gain acceptance as…
- a foot in both camps
- Rather than engaging in the *debate* on…, I would like to…
- Rather than adding yet another explanation for…, we would like instead to *focus* on…
- Rather than going over old ground,…
- In *contrast* to earlier studies,…
- In *contrast* to *previous research* on…, this study…
- Unlike some *or* many *or* most earlier studies, this study…
- This study contends that…
- This study questions the widely held view that *or* of…
- This study differs from *previous research* in a number of respects:
- At the risk of offending some readers,…

The limitations of current knowledge

- At present, little is known about…
- Very little is known about…
- There is as yet no clear *evidence* of *or* for…
- Little attention has been paid to…
- There has been as yet no systematic examination of…
- *Research* in this *area* has been limited to…
- …*research* has concentrated on…
- Very little has been written on *or* about…
- …is *or* are frequently overlooked in discussions of…
- …has rarely been done before
- …is not yet clearly *or* completely understood
- Our understanding to date has been limited to…
- …has received very little attention in the literature
- there is as yet *or* at present no consensus on…
- there is at present no general agreement on the causes of etc.…
- no satisfactory account *or* explanation of…has been given *or* provided
- this *diversity* of approaches *or* methods reflects…
- attempts to…have so far proved unsuccessful
- The initial claims that…were unduly *positive*
- *evaluation* is hindered *or* made more difficult by…
- It has not been demonstrated unequivocally *or* conclusively that…
- there are difficulties with all *or* a number of these explanations
- at least in its *or* their current *or* present form
- The question remains, however,…
- a *or* one *persistent* problem in…is…
- X and Y's results *posed* a number of questions which we have so far been unable to answer

Literature review and the relationship to other work

- Although much *important* work has been carried out on…, a number of questions remain.
- Although *considerable* progress has been made in…, many important *issues* remain *unexplored* or unresolved.
- Although much has been learned about…over the past…years, a number of *fundamental* questions remain.

Writing practice 10: Literature review and the relationship to other work

1. Using phrases from the section above, discuss how your study relates to other work

a. Describe your study's relationship to previous work

b. Discuss how your study relates to current work

c. Discuss any contrasting work

d. Outline the limitations of current knowledge – what is not known at present

2. Using the words in italics in the section above, write five new phrases for your text

3. In class, in groups or in pairs, exchange texts and evaluate each other's writing, going through the points above

11 Referring to other work

Remember to look up at the stars and not down at your feet...
Be curious. And however difficult life may seem,
there is always something you can do and succeed at
Stephen Hawking

The phrases in this section help you refer to other work. Referring to other work is termed *citing*. You can cite studies to support your point of view, or to show that you have read in your subject, for instance. Remember, if you cite an author word for word, you should use 'quotation marks': you should never copy someone else's work and make it appear as if it is your own – that is *plagiarism*, in other words academic theft.

- According to X,…
- X states…
- see X
- see for example X and Y
- see e.g. X
- see X, and also Y
- X believes that…
- X notes that…
- X observes that…
- X shows that…
- X adds that…
- X makes the point that…
- X puts the case for…
- X documents…
- As X states,…
- As X puts it,…
- as X explains:
- …, as X points out
- X describes this as…
- as discussed by X and Y
- as shown by X and Y
- as has been shown by X and Y
- as reported by X and *colleagues*
- as demonstrated in the work by X
- in a recent article by X
- in a paper *published* in…
- in her or his joint work with X
- see the *comments* by X
- In this article, X discusses…
- X, in a study of…, argues…
- X sees in…*evidence* for…
- …, citing for example…
- in a…*survey* of…by…
- …was or were reported to have…
- Following X,…
- …, as defined by X
- This follows X's study on…
- It seems best, following X, to…
- We have previously shown…
- We have shown in an earlier *publication*…
- in the same study…
- in a study of…*cited* by X
- a study conducted in…showed that…
- note for example the study or studies by X and Y
- X (personal *communication*)
- X (*forthcoming*)

- X (in press)
- originally *published* in…
- X (unpublished *data*)
- Figure courtesy of A. Smith.
- X's figure (after Shimizu et al. 2024) shows…

Citing work to support your view

- *Similar* findings were reported by X
- *Similar* findings have been reported in…
- Similarly, X and Y state…
- a *similar* point is made by X
- see for example the articles by X
- …has been described in…as…
- …is *similar* to figures or results etc. reported elsewhere (e.g. X et al.)
- …, which is *similar* to the figures or results etc. *obtained* by X
- support for this *interpretation* comes from…
- there is a growing body of *evidence* to suggest that…
- there is *considerable evidence* to support…
- there is now *considerable* or a great deal of *evidence* for…

- Additional support for this explanation etc. comes from…
- The results generally agree with those *obtained* in *previous* studies.
- As X suggests,…
- X also notes…
- …, as X also points out
- …, a point also made by X
- …, as X also states
- compare or cf. X's *comments* on…
- compare the *comments* by X on…
- compare X and Y who discuss…
- The study by X is probably closest to my own position
- …, though see also the *comments* by…
- contrast X's *comments* on…
- contrast the *comments* by X on…
- contrast X and Y who discuss…

Further references

- on…see X
- for further discussion see for example…
- see X for a *summary* of…
- For a *survey* or review of…, see X
- For a discussion of…, see X
- For a detailed examination of…, see X
- For a bibliography of studies on…, see X

Writing practice 11: Referring to other work

1. Using phrases from the section above, add a number of references in your text

a. Cite some work that supports your view

2. Using the words in italics in the section above, write five new phrases for your text

3. In class, in groups or in pairs, exchange texts and evaluate each other's writing, going through the points above

12 Reviewing other work

The great tragedy of Science
– the slaying of a beautiful hypothesis by an ugly fact
T. H. Huxley

Use the phrases in this and the following two sections to review other work.

- X's study of…
- X's 2024 paper on…
- X's 2024 study, entitled…, examines etc.…
- In a study of…, X…
- X's *investigation* of…
- X's discussion of…
- X and Y examine…
- X and Y examine or discuss in detail…
- X analyses GB or analyzes US…
- X's study looks at…
- X gives an overview of…
- The authors discuss…
- written from the standpoint of…
- The title of the study,…, suggests that…
- Topics covered or treated include…
- The *core* of X's argument is that…
- the study or X touches on a number of points
- one is immediately struck by…
- the arguments are *consistent* with an *approach* that…
- The study or their work, like that of…, is influenced by…
- The basic contention of…is that…
- a vigorous defence GB or defense US of…
- X's unorthodox *approach*
- X avoids this difficulty by…
- According to X and Y,…

- The authors argue that…
- X believes that…
- In X's view,…
- X attributes…to…
- X argues for…
- X and Y propose that…
- X's argument that…
- X advocates…
- The authors point out that…
- X *comments* on or that…
- X's observation that…
- X explains…as…
- X's point that…
- X compares…to…
- The authors point to the…
- X draws our attention to…
- X is careful to point out that…
- X is clearly *aware* of or that…
- The *author* is clearly very familiar with…
- The *author* demonstrates an intimate knowledge of…
- X also recognizes…
- …, as X states
- …, as X *indeed* points out
- …, as X makes clear
- The following quote illustrates…
- …, as the following quote illustrates:
- …is especially evident
- Typical *comments* by X are…

Reviewing other work

- It is clear from these *comments* that…
- From the *text* or article it is clear that…
- One reading of this would be…
- One *interpretation* of this would be…
- Reading between the lines,…
- It would be interesting to know or hear the author's thoughts on…
- a tacit assumption
- An assumption, *implicit* in X's argument, is…
- X and Y found that…
- X's *theory* reveals…
- X's *theory* demonstrates…
- X concludes from the *data* that…
- The most interesting finding relates to…
- It is interesting that…
- Without wishing to take sides,…
- to sit on the fence
- X has gone some way towards…
- X probably comes closest to…
- X's study raises a number of important *issues*
- The *issues* raised by X warrant further discussion
- The work challenges the assumption of or that…
- X's study or work departs radically from current thinking on…
- Clearly, if X's *theory* is correct, then…
- Although some have argued…,
- *significant* differences exist or remain between…and…
- In *contrast* to…, X sees the reason for…
- X's *theory* or explanation is perhaps preferable to Y's in that it…
- X and Y suggest instead that…
- X's *theory* is most plausible with regard to…
- X is clearly *aware* of the difficulties *involved* in…
- X rejects the view or idea that…
- X seeks to justify…
- X justifies this by…
- On the strength of this *evidence*, X argues that…
- X stops short of…
- X admits, however, that…
- X acknowledges that…
- X concedes that…
- *Overall*,…
- On balance,…

What you agree with

13 What you agree with

The superior person is broadminded but not partisan;
the inferior person is partisan but not broadminded
Confucius

You can use these phrases to write about what you agree with in another study or presentation.

- a useful introduction to…
- a valuable and important study of…
- an important and original work on…
- an important *contribution* to…
- a *positive contribution* to…
- an important *contribution* to recent work on…
- an important *contribution* to the *debate* on…
- The study makes several or a number of important contributions to…
- X's seminal work on…
- an authoritative study of…
- X writes with considerable *authority*: she or he…
- a *comprehensive* examination of…
- a standard work
- X's classic study of…
- X's study is a textbook example of…
- a valuable *contribution* to…
- valuable in its own right
- …is an achievement in itself
- X's work on…has come to be recognized as…
- X's work has had a profound influence on…
- X's *contribution* to…cannot be overestimated.
- detailed knowledge of…
- an in-depth discussion of…
- a well-researched *investigation* of…
- a thorough examination of…
- a lucid explanation of or for…
- a sophisticated *theory* of…
- elegant prose
- an elegant argument or model
- Of particular interest is X's finding etc. that…
- a new and interesting observation
- This is an interesting finding because it…
- the study contains a number of new and important *insights*:
- X and Y make a number of or several important observations
- The authors attempt, successfully in my or our view, to…
- X makes a number of valid points
- X makes a strong case for…
- X offers persuasive *evidence* for…
- a strong argument for…
- X's examination of…is exemplary
- X's treatment of…is particularly interesting or compelling
- X's *contribution* to…is clear
- X's study illustrates…
- X's study clearly demonstrates…
- X makes *explicit* the relationship between etc.…

- X makes a useful *distinction* between…and…
- As X *rightly* points out,…
- X states, in my view correctly, that…
- I or we share X's view of or that…
- It is possible to agree with X that…
- We broadly agree with X's *interpretation* of…

- X highlights a number of problems in current *theory*
- the main strength of X's argument is…
- the study breaks new ground
- ground-breaking *research* carried out last century
- The study is new in several respects:
- the study will be of particular interest to…

14 What you disagree with

Tact is the art of making a point without making an enemy
Isaac Newton

Use the phrases in this section to write about what you disagree with in another study or presentation. Informally, you may tell a family member or friend *You're wrong!* – but in academic writing or discussion you should express your criticism with tact – as Newton advises. The phrases below are all in an appropriate tone for academic English. By being less direct in your criticism, you appear more reasonable, and credible.

- It or the study lacks…
- The *author* appears to…
- X overlooks…
    - earlier studies of…
    - the existing literature on…
    - recent work on…
    - Y's findings…
    - important or *crucial data* on…
- X's study might *benefit* from…
- The study has, in my view, several shortcomings: firstly,…
- X seems to be unaware of…
- X ignores…
- X claims that…
- …, which X claims…

- X presupposes or assumes that…
- X's assertion that…
- It is curious that…
- It is *odd* that X does not mention…
- a puzzling statement
- the rather confusing statement that…
- …can hardly be viewed as…
- We believe this to be an *error*.
- Serious doubts have been raised about…
- a *fundamental* problem
- a further or unnecessary *layer* of complexity
- X fails to mention that…
- There is no reference to…
- Surprisingly, no mention is made of…

What you disagree with

- we are not told whether…
- The study fails to address the question…
- X pays scant attention to…
- to cut corners
- the *integrity* of the data
- anecdotal *evidence*
- ad hoc explanation
- dogmatic
- sweeping generalizations
- X's argument, point etc. that…
  - is too broad in *scope*
  - is too selective
  - is not new
- echoes of…
- Reading X, one is reminded of…
- …is merely reinventing the wheel

Their method

- X confuses…
- X and Y confuse the issue
- a misreading of…
- The authors underestimate…
- X and Y miss the point
- It is very much an oversimplification to…
- The authors fail to recognize…
- The disadvantage of this *approach* is that…
- A criticism of this explanation is that…
- …an incorrect assumption
- …unconvincing reasoning
- …inadequate controls
- …incorrectly assessed
- …merely *compounds* the problem
- X's argument contains a number of inconsistencies: firstly,…
- X's argument that…is flawed.
- X's explanation of or for…is unconvincing

- X's explanation of…is hardly convincing
- The author's claim that…is not well *founded*.
- the misleading statement that…
- It is *somewhat* of an overstatement or exaggeration to claim that…
- …contains a number of inaccuracies
- a number of controversial viewpoints
- In fact, the problem is more *complex*
- The *author* fails to take…into account
- X and Y take little or no account of…
- The authors have, however, failed to take account of…
- There is little or no systematic examination of…
- The study fails to answer the question of or whether…
- A problem with this argument is that…
- the same problem also applies to…
- There is little or no *evidence* to suggest that…

Their results or conclusions

- X's explanation depends on or relies on…
- The *evidence* for…is inconclusive
- The reasoning here is problematic
- the conclusions are *somewhat* weak
- X's arguments…are unconvincing
- this, however, holds only for…
- the claim or argument that…simply does not hold water
- …is not *sufficient* argument for the existence of etc.…
- this assumption is rather *arbitrary*, however

What you disagree with

- X's main assumption that…is debatable or problematic
- We would dispute X's *conclusion* that…
- X's explanation for or of…is rather or highly speculative
- this *contradiction* has also been pointed out by X
- an *error* in the calculation
- X's figures, results, conclusions etc. should, however, be treated with caution
- The results should be treated with a degree of or some or *considerable* caution
- X's conclusions would carry more weight if…
- further clarification of…is *required*
- X and Y fail to explain…
- the causal relationship between…and…needs to be clarified
- a number of valid criticisms
- …violates the *principle* of…
- This invalidates, however,…
- X's argument rests or depends almost entirely on…
- X's statement or *theory* etc.…requires some qualification
- X gives a detailed if not always tenable *analysis* of…
- X attempts, unsuccessfully in my or our view, to…
- Where X's argument or explanation falls down is in…
- X's explanation is not implausible, if not entirely satisfactory
- Further *research* is necessary to establish a clearer relationship between…and…
- Further *research* is necessary before ascribing…to…
- A more complete explanation of…would…
- a simplistic assumption

Your view

- My own view is that…
- a number of reservations
- One cause for concern is…
- It is not necessarily the case that…
- It does not necessarily follow that…
- …begs the question…
- One may question whether…
- To claim here that…
- …would be denying the fact that…
- X claims, in my view wrongly, that…
- the question is rather…
- it is more likely that…
- The point is surely rather that…
- One could in fact also state that…
- it would be more *accurate* to say that…
- a more promising *approach* would be…
- a more plausible explanation would be that…
- It is important to make a *distinction* between…
- It is important to distinguish between…and…
- If the most important etc. factor had been…, then it would be expected that…
- The *author* has clearly not understood…
- The authors merely pay lip service to…
- The paper offers little in the way of…
- The paper offers little that is new.
- The study offers only cursory examination of…

What you disagree with

- we should beware of throwing out the baby with the bathwater
- While acknowledging the author's *contribution*,…
- While a valuable *contribution* in many respects,…
- At the risk of offending…,
- pace X

- …must be examined more closely
- …cannot be accepted as it stands
- more needs to be said about…
- However, given these reservations,…
- *Despite* these reservations,…
- *Despite* these limitations,…
- Given these qualifications,…

Writing practice 12–14: Reviewing other work

1. Using phrases from the sections above, review a paper or book in your subject

a. Write about what you agree with in the work

b. Write about what you disagree with

2. Using the words in italics in the section above, write five new phrases for your text

3. In class, in groups or in pairs, exchange texts and evaluate each other's writing, going through the points above

15 Arguing your case and putting forward ideas

If I have a thousand ideas and only one turns out to be good,
I am satisfied
Alfred Nobel

You can use the phrases in this section to argue your case and put forward ideas. *Arguing your case* means giving evidence to support your opinion.

- My own view is that…
- In our view,…
- This study argues the importance of…
- the reason for this is…
- Arguably,…
- from a or an…point of view
- from this *perspective*
- from a…standpoint
- our contention is that…
- At issue here is or are…
- This point is particularly *relevant* to…
- an important point to bear in mind
- A *couple* of points are worth mentioning here: firstly,…
- …is or are important to the explanation of…
- In view of this, it is also important to examine…
- What I or we wish to emphasize here…
- It should be emphasized that…
- Detailed examination of…reveals…
- This becomes clear when one examines…
- It is by no means an exaggeration to state that…
- It is true that…
- What is certain is that…
- *logic* would suggest that…

- It is *obvious* that…
- It is self-evident that…
- compelling *evidence* of or for…
- The decisive *evidence* for…
- It is certainly true that…
- There is no doubt that…
- It is undoubtedly the case that…
- There can be little doubt that…
- We are or remain *convinced* that…
- The *justification* for this assumption etc. is that…
- …, which demonstrates that…can indeed…
- It follows that…
- Hence, we can say that…
- …*thereby* demonstrating or showing clearly that…
- It is clear that…
- …clearly…
- Obviously,…
- Not surprisingly,…
- note that…
- A valid point is that…
- It is widely accepted that…
- Common sense suggests that…
- This strongly suggests that…
- It seems clear that…

Arguing your case and putting forward ideas

- this is largely or mainly a or the result of...
- Without disregarding the importance of...,...
- It is possible, however, that...
- We can *assume* that...
- It is quite possible that...
- It may well be the case that...
- It is worth noting that...
- It is important to point out that...
- a more likely *interpretation* is that...
- ...or, more plausibly,...
- a different line of reasoning
- While this proposal may seem *radical*, we believe that it offers a number of advantages.
- ...in support of...
- strong support for this *interpretation* of...as...comes from...
- indirect support for...comes from...
- There is indirect *evidence* of...
- This lends weight to the argument that...
- This strengthens the argument...
- This is *confirmed* by...
- This is borne out by...
- ...is further supported by...
- Indeed,...
- indeed, one could say that...
- in other words
- ..., i.e....
- To put it another way,...
- Put another way,...
- More specifically,...
- To reiterate:...
- *Furthermore*,...
- Note also that...
- It is equally clear that...
- This clearly requires a...
- This is not to say that...
- This raises the question whether...
- This raises questions about the *validity* of...
- This raises another issue
- This raises a further question:
- I do not wish to imply that...

Writing practice 15: Arguing your case and putting forward ideas

1. Using the phrases above, write a section in your text or presentation arguing your case

2. Using the words in italics in the section above, write five new phrases for your text or talk

3. In class, in groups or in pairs, evaluate each other's writing or presentations, going through the points above

16 Arguing against

Those who know that the consensus of many centuries has sanctioned the conception that the earth remains at rest in the middle of the heavens... would...regard it as...insane...if I made the opposite assertion that the earth moves
Copernicus

The phrases in this section help you argue against an opposing point of view.

- neither...nor...
- This does not imply that...
- ...begs the question...
- One question is whether...
- It is questionable or doubtful whether...
- It is by no means clear that...
- This raises the question whether...
- We can question whether in fact...
- While it may well be true that...,...
- While it may well be valid that...,...
- While we cannot *deny* that..., we...
- ...inconclusive *evidence*
- ...insufficient proof
- ...discouraging results
- ...unsatisfactory results
- to outline the case against...
- it is important to consider...
- it is important to take account of...
- it is important not to overlook that...
- the *evidence* for...is sketchy at best
- ...fails to take...into account...
- ...is or are frequently overlooked in discussion of...
- It is frequently overlooked that...
- Although...may play an important *role*, it is clearly not the only factor.
- The problem, however, is that...
- It does not follow that...
- One difficulty is...
- a or the lack of...
- it does not easily explain...
- Difficulties arise in...
- ...poses particular problems in cases where...
- the problems *identified* also apply to...
- A further problem is...
- A *potential* problem is...
- This is further complicated by...
- A or the flaw in this argument is that...
- A more serious failing is that...
- A or one *major* weakness of...is...
- A serious drawback with or of this *approach* is...
- One of the *prime* failings of this *theory* or explanation etc. is...
- The or one problem with this explanation or *approach* etc. is that...
- A serious question remains concerning...
- Serious doubts have been raised about...
- However, there is also *evidence* of or for...
- However, there is also *evidence* to suggest that...
- It is probable, therefore, that...reflects or represents...rather than...
- It is by no means the case that...

Arguing against

- …the present study indicates that this is not the case.
- It is frequently claimed that…; however,…
- Although many authors would agree that…,…
- From a…standpoint, however,…
- Crucially, however,…
- However, it would be rash to conclude from this that…
- However, we cannot be certain that or whether…
- The *relevant* or important factor here is not…, rather…
- However, none of the explanations accounts for…
- The explanation simply does not hold water.
- An *alternative* explanation would be…
- a more likely *interpretation* is that…

Writing practice 16: Arguing against

1. Using phrases from the section above, take an assertion in your subject and argue why you disagree with it

2. Using the words in italics in the section above, write five new phrases for your text or talk

3. In class, in groups or in pairs, evaluate each other's writing or presentations, going through the points above

17 Analysis and discussion

Information is not knowledge
Albert Einstein

The section below gives you phrases for analysis and discussion.

- to examine…
- to examine…more closely
- to observe…
- to observe…in detail
- to evaluate…
- to assess…
- to assess the significance of…
- In determining…,…
- to determine whether…
- whether or not…
- We observed…
- By analysing GB or analyzing US…,
- …was analysed GB or analyzed US by or for…
- The *analysis* here is based on…
- It is relatively easy to describe…
- one immediately *obvious* feature of…is…
- A quick glance at…shows that…
- …*exhibit* classic signs or symptoms of…
- From…it is *apparent* that…
- …is immediately *apparent*
- …is most pronounced in…
- …shows *evidence* of…
- Superficially at least,…
- *Underlying*…is the view etc. that…
- *Analysis* of the *data revealed*…
- Closer examination of…reveals that…
- Closer *inspection* revealed that…
- *Viewed* in this way,…
- There is some indication that…
- Observations of…suggest that…
- The presence of…can be tested by…
- An important test for…is whether or not…
- …may be or is *confirmed* by…
- …tends to *occur* or be found in…
- …is not a necessary condition for…
- the *interaction* of…and…
- *exposure* to…results in…
- One way of examining or viewing…
- One way of analysing GB or analyzing US…
- …can be thought of as…
- Comparison of theoretical predictions with actual observations *revealed* that…

Characteristics

- the type of…
- the size of…
- The *dimensions* of…are or were as follows:
- the level of…
- the degree of…
- the extent of…
- the *intensity* of…
- the presence of…
- the absence of…
- the properties of…
- the nature of…
- the *core* of…

Analysis and discussion

- the nucleus of…
- the *role* of…
- a change of or in…
- a change or *shift* from…to…
- a gradual *process* of…
- …typical of…
- …consists of…
- …is made up of…
- …is composed of…
- …is determined by…
- …is governed by…
- …is subject to…
- …is a *function* of…
- …is independent of…
- …is characteristic of…
- …is characterized by…
- …is an indicator of…
- …is the best indicator of…
- …is a good or reliable indicator of…
- …may also be present in…
- …can be described as…
- a typical case of…
- a textbook case of…
- an interesting aspect of…is…
- one important feature of…is…
- a number of *physical* features
- a *significant* feature of…
- a *fundamental* characteristic of…
- an *integral* part of…
- …is an essential component of…
- …is or are associated with…
- …comprises a number of *components*
- the or one *dominant* feature of…is…
- *features* of both…and…
- …has or plays a dual *role* in…
- …shows a number of typical or unusual features
- the *structure* of…is revealed by
- the *site* of…
- The main or chief characteristics of…are…
- One important characteristic of…is…
- the common denominator is…
- these *features* are characteristic of…
- One of the characteristics of…is what X has termed or called…
- …can be grouped under a number of different types
- Difficulties arise in attempting to characterize…as…

Discussion

- The importance of…is demonstrated by the fact that…
- …assumes a special significance because or as…
- One of the most *obvious consequences* of…is
- the or an important observation that…
- A point that can be made is that…
- This may be discussed in terms of…
- …is perhaps best viewed as…
- If this is the case, then…
- If, for the sake of argument, we *assume*…
- …can be deduced from…
- This attests to…
- This agrees with…
- …is or are, in effect,…
- …supports the *notion* that…
- …may be *inferred* from…
- This would suggest that…
- There is some *evidence* to suggest that…
- A clue to…can be or is found in…
- A clue to…lies in the fact that…

Analysis and discussion

- It may be argued that…
- This may be applicable to…
- the extent to which this reflects…is unclear
- a real if elusive relationship between…
- to tip the scales in favour GB or favor US of…
- the *distinction* between…and…is not always clear cut
- a *bias* towards…
- a relatively weak predictor
- …is a poor predictor of…
- …is often masked by…
- …leads to overrepresentation or underrepresentation of…
- systematic differences in…
- It is not *obvious* how or why…
- It is by no means clear that…
- The question arises whether…
- It is an open question whether…
- This raises a further question:
- This raises the issue whether…
- This raises a number of questions.
- The *notion* that or of…raises a number of *fundamental* or important questions for…
- …cannot simply be explained by or as…
- This raises questions about the *validity* of…

Writing practice 17: Analysis and discussion

1. Using phrases from the section above, examine and discuss the central points of your text or presentation

2. Write and present a poster on your work, either individually or in groups or pairs

3. Using the words in italics in the section above, write five new phrases for your text or talk

4. In class, in groups or in pairs, evaluate each other's writing or presentations, going through the points above

18 Explaining and giving reasons

*If you can't explain it simply,
you don't understand it well enough*
Albert Einstein

As Einstein advises, try to make your explanation as lucid – clear and easy to understand – as possible.

- This explains why…
- This is because…
- …is self-explanatory
- …essential to the explanation of…
- This can be explained as…
- …can be explained by…
- This explanation also accounts for…
- the most likely explanation
- Many…can be explained by or as…
- …is or are better explained by or as…
- …is accounted for by…
- …, which accounts for…
- An or one explanation for or of…is that…
- A likely explanation for…is…
- …important to the explanation of…
- …can only be adequately explained by…
- …accounts for a considerable number of cases of…
- This in part explains…
- This may explain…
- This would explain why…
- Other possible explanations or causes are…
- An alternative explanation would be…
- One possible explanation for…is…
- A more plausible explanation for…would be that…
- This explanation would appear to be supported by…
- By adopting the view of or that…, we can explain…
- a factor in…
- an important factor in…
- the importance of…as a factor in…
- a contributory factor
- a number of external factors
- this factor may contribute to…
- …plays an important part in…
- …plays a crucial role in…
- …has an important role in…
- the key to the problem
- one solution might be…
- the main cause of…is…
- the primary cause of…
- …is one of the most common causes of…in…
- …can be shown to be…
- the motivation for or behind…
- The fundamental reason for…is clear:
- the principal reason for…
- For this or that reason…
- one reason for…
- one of the reasons for…
- As already discussed, one reason for the…

Explaining and giving reasons

- for a number of reasons
- The reason for…is unknown, but…has been suggested by X as a possible factor.
- The key to understanding…is…
- *crucial* to the understanding of…
- can be best understood by or as…
- This highlights the importance of…
- one example of the importance or relevance of…
- This demonstrates…
- therefore
- i.e.
- Clearly,…
- …can be seen in a number of developments or examples
- This is as true for…as it is for…
- It is frequently the case that…
- It is also important to note that…
- One point worth noting here is that…
- On the basis of this…,
- Indeed, in many cases…
- This is *consistent* with…
- as a means of…
- …associated with…
- …, which is based on the idea of…
- *features* or developments etc. compatible with…
- This does not, however, explain…
- This cannot explain…
- …is or are difficult to explain because of…
- This explanation is *adequate*, if not entirely satisfactory.
- the reasons for…are *complex*
- This explanation is barely *adequate*
- None of these explanations accounts for the…

Writing practice 18: Explaining and giving reasons

1. Using phrases from the section above, explain the main points of your text or presentation

a. Give reasons for your view

2. Using the words in italics in the section above, write five new phrases for your text or talk

3. In class, in groups or in pairs, evaluate each other's writing or presentations, going through the points above

19 Qualifying and hedging

> 'When I use a word,' Humpty Dumpty said, in a rather scornful tone,
> 'it means just what I choose it to mean – neither more nor less'
> 'The question is,' said Alice, 'whether you can make words mean so many different things'
> Lewis Carroll

Qualifying has the common meaning of achieving a required standard, for example to qualify as a doctor. In academic writing, it has an additional meaning of adding a proviso, condition or limit to a generalization. Hedging means expressing your opinion less stridently.

- if…
- whether…
- If…, then…
- If this is the case, then…
- This depends on…
- …, depending on…
- either…or…
- neither…nor…
- …, but…
- However,…
- …nor, however,…
- Although…,
- …rather…
- rather than…
- though
- Unfortunately,…
- At the same time,…
- …, albeit…
- regardless of…
- …not necessarily…
- Nevertheless,…
- In fact,…
- In reality,…
- Of course,…
- Generally speaking,…
- Broadly speaking,…

- In large part, this is due to…
- in many respects
- In practice,…
- In principle,…
- Ideally,…
- providing or provided that…
- …with the proviso that…
- a condition of…
- …is a necessary condition for…
- …is a prerequisite of…
- …unless stated otherwise
- in all probability
- to all intents and purposes
- frequently
- on the whole
- a wide range of…
- a variety of…
- by no means uncommon
- in a broader sense
- with one or two exceptions
- …was confined to…
- …are found predominantly in…
- …is or are more likely to be
- a number of…
- some…
- probably

Qualifying and hedging

- in some cases
- to some extent
- at least to some extent
- at least in part
- partly…, and partly…
- in some sense
- It is possible that…
- possibly
- perhaps
- under these *circumstances*
- in this respect
- in this case
- specifically,…
- Strictly speaking,…
- only
- relatively few cases of…
- with minor exceptions
- very few cases of…
- *solely*
- with little or no…
- with the exception of…
- a notable exception
- a number of reservations
- To my knowledge,…
- There are, to our knowledge, no…
- There are no *objective* grounds for…
- It should be noted that…
- It is worth bearing in mind that…
- It is important to bear in mind that…
- It should, *nevertheless*, be borne in mind that…
- It is easy to underestimate the…
- It is important not to ignore…
- It is equally clear that…
- While it may seem unlikely that…, it is important to remember that…
- Although it may well be true that…, it is important not to overlook…
- Although it may be the case that…, it is important to bear in mind…
- Although it is generally accepted that…,…
- without jumping to conclusions
- However, this is not to say that…
- …, though the fact that…
- …should not be understood as…
- …should not be underestimated
- …cannot be ruled out
- …does not necessarily imply that…
- …can be better accounted for by or as…
- …, though it must be emphasized that…
- While we are unable to *guarantee*…, we are able to state that…
- *Furthermore*, it is by no means the case that…
- Leaving aside where this is not the case etc., we can say that…
- While the findings are promising,…
- It is certainly possible that…
- It is certainly true that…; however,…
- While there is no question that…,…
- While it may well be true that…,…
- Up to a point, this may be true; however,…
- While this may be true to some extent,…
- While this may be valid in some cases,…
- the figures, results etc. should be treated with caution
- we should or must be cautious about generalizing…
- there is more than one possible development, explanation etc.
- Although this does not exclude the possibility that…, it does suggest that other *factors* may be *relevant*.

Qualifying and hedging

- *Similar* results have been recorded elsewhere, *albeit* in a different *context*.
- a balance must be drawn between…
- it is a difference of degree, not of kind
- …represents not so much…, but…
- other contributory *factors* may also be *relevant*
- This is due to a combination of *factors* rather than *solely* attributable to…
- A widely held assumption is that…; however,…
- However, it cannot be denied that…
- This does not mean, however, that…
- This does not necessarily mean…
- The principles discussed here cannot, however, be taken as absolute.
- The extent to which *factors* such as…are *significant* varies.
- …is just one aspect of the problem
- a number of limitations
- not wholly *accurate*
- It is impossible to…
- It is not possible to…
- It is debatable or questionable whether…
- to what extent this is *parallel* to…is unclear
- the extent to which this reflects…is unclear
- On first glance this may appear promising, but…
- …seems at first sight…; however,…
- While superficially appealing,…does not stand up to closer scrutiny
- closer examination reveals, however,…
- The results should be treated with great caution
- While promising, further work needs to be carried out before…
- …needs to be more *explicit*
- The limitations of…become evident if one considers…
- …very little *evidence* for or of…
- …would carry more weight if…
- An *alternative* explanation is that…
- It is not necessarily the case that…
- …this is by no means always the case
- It is by no means the case that…
- It would be wrong to *assume* that…
- It is unlikely that…
- It is rarely the case that…
- examples of…are rare
- examples of…are few and far between
- This *process*, type etc. is *restricted* to…
- Of a total of…, only…
- the exception rather than the rule
- It remains to be seen whether…

Writing practice 19: Qualifying and hedging

1. Using phrases from the section above, qualify your findings or conclusions

2. Using the words in italics in the section above, write five new phrases for your text

3. In class, in groups or in pairs, exchange texts and evaluate each other's writing, going through the points above

20 Quantifying

Life is finite
While knowledge is infinite
Zhuangzi

The phrases in this section help you write about quantities, including measurement, amount, order and change.

Measurement

- to measure…
- to calculate…
- to determine…
- to compute…
- to count…
- to quantify…
- to weigh…
- to weigh up…
- to gauge…
- to *estimate*…
- to establish…
- the number of…
- the size of…
- the magnitude of the problem
- the *volume* of…
- the *capacity* of…
- the amount of…
- the degree of…
- the level of…
  - a high level of…
  - high levels of…
  - moderate levels of…
  - a low level of…
  - low levels of…
- the rate of…
  - at a rate of…
- a high rate of…
- a low rate of…
- the value of…
- the true cost of…
- the occurrence of…
- the frequency of…
- the *incidence* of…
- the *concentration* of…
- the composition of…
- the extent of…
- the percentage of…
- the *proportion* of…
- the *ratio* of…
- the estimated number of…
- the presence or absence of…
- the existence of…
- a group of…
- a quota
- an *estimate* of…
- a value for…
- the *sum* of…
- the combined total of…
- the total number of…
- …was or were measured by or with…
- …was or were calculated as or by…
- …was or were calculated as follows:
- …was or were determined as follows:
- Using…, we calculated…

Quantifying

- Calculations show…
- to use…as a yardstick to measure the…
- to miscalculate…
- to misjudge…
- to overestimate…
- to underestimate…
- a *minimum* requirement is that…

Amount

- exactly
- precisely
- *virtually*
- almost
- nearly
- approximately
- an approximation
- We have *approximated* the figures to…
- roughly
- Roughly speaking,…
- in the order of…
- by and large
- within…
- within the *range*…
- Within this *range* lie…
- numerous
- countless
- innumerable
- the vast majority of…
- a full *complement* of…
- the *maximum* possible…is…
- in all but…
- most, if not all, of…
- the lion's share of…
- a large number of…
- a high percentage of…
- a great deal of…
- much of…

- up to ten different types etc.…
- a *significant* number of…
- a *considerable* number of…
- at amounts etc. exceeding…
- at levels etc. in excess of…
- over 50% or *percent* of…
- at least
- …equal to…
- …equates to…
- *equivalent* to…
- of equal value
- in equilibrium
- proportional to…
- to balance
- …is *offset* by…
- On average,…
- to differ
- to diverge
- to deviate from…
- to disagree with…
- inversely proportional to…
- …accounted for approximately…*percent* of cases
- several…
- some…
- less or fewer than 50% or *percent* of…
- a fraction of…
- at most
- Of these,…
- Of the…examined or tested etc.,…
- Of these, only about…*involved*…
- Of a total of…, only…
- a small number of…
- a limited number of…
- the remaining…
- the remainder of…
- little or no…
- very few…

Quantifying

- the scarcity of…
- a or the lack of…
- a dearth of…
- an absence of…

Order

- hierarchy
- level
- position
- in order of…
- in alphabetical order
- in chronological order
- in numerical order
- in the following order:
- in *sequence*
- arranged in order of…
- ranked according to…
- graded according to…
- …can be rated as follows:
- *intermediate* between…and…
- more than…
- greater than…
- over 95% or *percent* of…
- much larger than…
- …peaked at…
- …was consistently higher than…
- …was significantly higher in…than in…
- greater than *normal*
- higher than expected
- above average
- progressively larger or smaller
- cumulative
- less than…
- considerably smaller than…
- lower than *normal*
- less than *predicted*
- …was significantly lower…
- under 5% or *percent*
- below average
- substandard

Change

- to change
- a change of…
- to modify
- to revise
- to adjust
- to *alter*
- to transform
- the or a *transition* from…to…
- a *shift* from…to…
- this *dramatic* shift from…to…
- to substitute…for…
- a *transformation* of…from…to…
- to convert…into…
- we *converted*…from…to…
- to vary
- the number of…varies
- to fluctuate
- such *fluctuations* in…are normal or unusual
- to alternate between…and…
- to expand…
- to enlarge…
- to extend…
- to intensify…
- to multiply…
- to magnify…
- to strengthen…
- to raise…
- to boost…
- to double…
- to triple…
- to quadruple…

Quantifying

- twofold
- threefold
- fourfold
- a or the rise in…

- an increase of…
- There was an increase in…
- There is or was a clear increase or decrease in…
- the greatest increase was in…
- …increased significantly
- …increased the rate of…

- …was or were increased by…*percent*
- to maximize
- to round up…
- to round down…
- a decrease in or of…
- the greatest decrease occurred in…
- …decreased significantly
- …was reduced from…to…
- a fall in…
- a reduction in the rate of…
- to minimize
- …declined markedly

Writing practice 20: Quantifying

1. Using phrases from the section above, quantify any data in your text. Discuss its

a. Measurement

b. Amount

c. Order

d. Change

2. Using the words in italics in the section above, write five new phrases for your text

3. In class, in groups or in pairs, exchange texts and evaluate each other's writing, going through the points above

21 Time

Make use of time,
Let not advantage slip
William Shakespeare

The phrases in this section help you write about time, including duration, frequency, present, past and future.

- the start or beginning of…
- the onset of…
- the end of…
- at any time
- at any given time
- at any one time
- the first stage of…
- *concurrent*
- simultaneous
- a *contemporary* account of…
- Shakespeare's etc. *contemporary*
- consecutive
- in chronological order
- the *project* was completed on time

Duration

- between…and…
- from…to…
- an *interval* of…seconds, hours etc.
- over the course of…five weeks, one year etc.
- a 24-hour *period*
- for or during the entire *period*
- during the study
- for the *duration* of the experiment
- to change over time
- to evolve over time

- a *brief period* of…
- a rapid development
- a *time* of rapid change
- a swift decision to…
- a continuous *process* of…
- chronic poverty, illness etc.
- a *temporary* measure
- …is only a short-term solution to…
- …has been plagued by short-termism
- a long-term problem
- long-term change proved to be more difficult…
- a or one *persistent* problem in…is…
- …*eventually* led to…
- in the long run
- a permanent solution
- The problem was *eventually* solved by…
- a *period* of *stability* or great change
- the…*period* is usually defined as…
- the Elizabethan etc. era is or was characterized by…
- …spans several decades or centuries
- an age of…
- a new epoch
- the end of an epoch

Time

Frequency

- the occurrence of…
- the frequency of…
- the rate of…
- the *incidence* of…
- always
- without fail
- frequently
- repeatedly
- in quick succession
- a succession of…
- …recurs over and again
- time and again
- time after time
- often
- regularly
- at regular intervals
- at 1, 10, 30 etc. minute intervals
- every 5 etc. minutes, seconds, years etc.
- a five-year *cycle*
- per second
- per minute
- per hour
- hourly
- per week
- weekly
- per month
- monthly
- per annum
- annually
- an *annual* increase of…
- yearly
- sometimes
- occasionally
- hardly
- seldom
- rarely
- never

Present

- now
- the present day
- The situation today is that…
- the *status* of…
- At present, we are unable to…
- at the moment
- current *theory*, knowledge, methods, trends etc.
- currently
- until now
- Recently,…
- recent developments in…
- as recently as…
- Until recently, very little was known about…
- …is a relatively recent *phenomenon*
- To date, very few examples of…have been found

Previous and past

- at the outset
- from the outset
- from the start
- before
- *prior* to…
- Previously,…
- *previous* experiments have been unsuccessful in…
- an early sign or indication of…
- …was noticeable early on
- As stated earlier,…
- in the past
- already in…
- two weeks, months, years etc. ago
- over…ago

Time

- less than…ago
- circa…
- since the 1950s etc.
- by the end of the nineteenth century
- at the end of the sixteenth century
- an or the era of…
- …dates from…
- We can date…to…
- This *method*, though dated, has a number of advantages
- …is now obsolete

Subsequent and future

- after
- immediately after
- soon after
- after a further 3 minutes etc.
- the future of…is uncertain
- in…days, months, years etc.
- on *schedule*
- the *project* is on *schedule*
- …is scheduled or due to be completed in…
- to postpone
- at a later stage
- to be on the verge of…
- the *predicted* results
- at the *forthcoming conference* on…
- modern architecture, art etc.
- a new *generation* of…
- X was ahead of her or his time
- X's work, paper etc. *anticipated* the development, discovery etc. of…

Writing practice 21: Time

1. Using phrases from the section above, discuss any aspect of time in your text. Consider the following:

a. Duration
b. Frequency
c. Present
d. Previous and past
e. Subsequent and future

2. Using the words in italics in the section above, write five new phrases for your text

3. In class, in groups or in pairs, exchange texts and evaluate each other's writing, going through the points above

22 Hypotheses and probability

> *The grand aim of all science*
> *[is] to cover the greatest number of empirical facts by logical deduction*
> *from the smallest possible number of hypotheses or axioms*
> Albert Einstein

The phrases in this section help you state a hypothesis and discuss probability. *Hypo* comes from the Greek word for 'under'. A hypothesis is therefore an idea, explanation or theory that is not yet final.

- Theoretically,…
- In *theory*,…
- In *principle*,…
- an *abstract* argument
- a model of or for…
- According to the model,…
- …may be *inferred* from…
- …has a strong theoretical basis
- Hypothetically,…
- a hypothetical question
- to construct a *hypothesis*
- to formulate a *hypothesis*
- The *hypothesis* can be stated as follows:
- A *hypothesis* could be made that…
- …has led to the *hypothesis* that…is caused by…
- a working *hypothesis*
- the *underlying hypothesis* that…
- an *alternative hypothesis* or proposition that…
- a *series* of hypotheses predicting…
- to evaluate the *hypothesis* that…
- to test the *hypothesis* that…
- We tested the *hypothesis* by…
- We are able to *refine* our hypothesis

- to verify a *hypothesis*
- the *hypothesis* is *confirmed* by…
- …supports the *hypothesis* that…
- …refutes or disproves the *hypothesis* that…

Possibility

- It is entirely possible that…
- It is possible that…
- One possibility is…
- One possible *theory* is that…
- A further possibility is…
- Yet another possibility is…
- the possibility of…
- the likelihood of…
- One way of viewing…
- It is not inconceivable that…
- It is possible to argue that…
- a possible explanation for…
- It may well be the case that…
- It seems likely that…
- …more likely
- …less likely
- …may be associated with…

Hypotheses and probability

- whether…is attributable to…
- There are a number of possible *outcomes*

Suggestion and speculation

- This suggests that…
- One suggestion might be that…
- …may be due to…
- It may be that…
- This may *indicate*…
- This may reflect…
- The most likely explanation for or of…is…
- A number of tentative conclusions can be drawn
- Provisionally,…
- One solution might be…
- One *alternative* might be…
- One tentative proposal might be…
- One *scenario* is that…
- the *potential* effects of…on…
- It is possible to speculate that…
- One may speculate whether…
- an educated guess
- Another suggestion might be…
- This finding has prompted the plausible speculation that…
- This has led some authors to suggest that…
- This has led some authors to speculate whether…
- One suggestion, though purely conjecture, might be that…
- In the absence of…, we can only speculate on…
- Explanations of or for…remain highly speculative.

Probability and prediction

- the probability that or of…
- …is probably due to…
- the most probable explanation
- It is highly probable that…
- Potentially,…
- We *estimate* that…
- Estimates suggest that…
- Predictably,…
- As forecast,…
- we would predict that…
- projections *range* from…to…
- …tends or tend to…
- …tends or tend to *occur* or be found in…
- a or the tendency to…
- it is or was inevitable that…
- …would *inevitably* follow
- The results were predictable
- …was or were widely *predicted*
- The results are or were as *predicted*

Assumption and implication

- assuming that…
- an assumption that…
- to take for *granted*
- If we *assume* that…
- If, for the sake of argument, we *assume*…
- based on the assumption that…
- the assumptions that underpin…
- This assumption is supported by…
- …may support the assumption that…
- This is presumably due to…
- …, presumably because of…
- We may surmise that…
- If…, then…
- If this is the case, then…

Hypotheses and probability

- It follows that if…, then…
- this *implies* that…
- By implication,…
- The implication is that…
- the *implications* of…

- …may have a number of important *implications* for…
- …has *widespread implications*
- This can be expressed by or as the following implicational statement:

Writing practice 22: Hypotheses and probability

1. Using phrases from the section above, put forward a hypothesis

a. Discuss the probability of your hypothesis

2. Using the words in italics in the section above, write five new phrases for your text or talk

3. In class, in groups or in pairs, evaluate each other's writing or presentations, going through the points above

23 Rhetorical questions and addressing your audience

I keep six honest serving-men, they taught me all I knew
Their names are What and Why and When, and How and Where and Who
Rudyard Kipling

A rhetorical question is a question you ask your reader or listener – but answer yourself. Rhetorical questions and addressing your audience are ways of engaging your readers or listeners by involving them in your paper or presentation.

- Consider, for example,…
- Now consider the issue of…
- Note that…
- Recall that…
- many readers…
- the majority of readers
- the question why…
- This raises the question…
- This brings us to the question of…
- One may well ask whether…?
- One might ask, for example, whether…?
- The question can be asked whether…
- What can we say about…?
- What does this tell us about…?
- What is the explanation for this?
- What is the *role* of…?

- What *evidence* is there for…?
- How are…related?
- How can…be expressed?
- How might…be explained?
- How can we understand…?
- In what way is…currently understood?
- How can these different or various approaches be reconciled?
- Can we replicate the theoretical results empirically?
- What conclusions can be drawn from this?
- The question why…appears to have no simple answer or solution.
- This explanation etc. would, for many scholars, be unacceptable.

Writing practice 23: Rhetorical questions and addressing your audience

1. Using phrases from the section above, address the reader of your text or audience of your presentation

   a. Add one or two rhetorical questions

2. Using the words in italics in the section above, write five new phrases for your text

3. In class, in groups or in pairs, evaluate each other's writing or presentations, going through the points above

24 Comparing and contrasting

*Acquire new knowledge whilst thinking over the old,
and you may become a teacher of others*
Confucius

Use the phrases in this section to compare and contrast – for example whether two or more things are equal or equivalent, the same or similar, and the relationship between them.

- Firstly, secondly, thirdly…
- (a), (b), (c)…
- (i), (ii), (iii)…
- On the one hand…, on the other hand…
- both…, and…
- as well as…
- not only…, but also…
- …or, for that matter,…
- Just as…,…
- Comparison of…
- compared with or to…
- To give a comparison from…,
- …has been compared or likened to…
- …is or are often compared to or with…
- …are broadly comparable
- comparatively few
- relatively speaking
- It is interesting to compare…
- For comparison, we also examined…
- Comparison of…*revealed* that…
- The results were compared with or to those *obtained* in or by…
- a comparative study or *investigation* of…

Equal or equivalent

- …equals…
- …is equal to…
- …is *equivalent* to…
- to equate…with…
- the terms…and…are used interchangeably
- Equally,…
- It is equally clear that…
- in equilibrium
- On balance,…
- to strike a balance between…and…
- in *parallel*
- …parallels…
- …is paralleled by…
- a *parallel process* of…

Same or similar

- *identical* to…
- almost or *virtually identical*
- the same as…
- …bears a striking resemblance to…
- …is *virtually* indistinguishable from…
- There is an *obvious* resemblance between…
- the difference is only *marginal*
- the results were *relatively uniform*
- This is also true of or for…
- The same is true of or for…
- The same applies to…

Comparing and contrasting

- The same principles that determine, govern etc....apply to...
- much the same as...
- in much the same way as...
- the same seems to be true of...
- *similar* to...
- ...approximates to...
- ...similarly shows...
- *similar* cases etc. *occur* in...
- ...shows a *similar* pattern to...
- the similarity between...
- a *similar* type or kind of...
- Similarly, for example,...
- there are many similarities between...and...
- there is a great deal of similarity between...and...
- In several or some respects,...is closer to...than to...
- ...has or have much in common with...
- ...mimics...
- to duplicate the results *obtained* by or in...
- *Likewise*,...
- the analogy of...
- By analogy,...
- an *analogous* case is when or where...
- ...closely resembles...
- ...resembles...more than...

Relation

- in relation to...
- relative to...
- ...is or are related to...
- ...correlates with...
- the correlation of...with...
- a or the correlation between...
- ...are clearly closely connected or related
- The *link* between...and...is obvious or unproven
- relatively speaking
- the relative merits of...
- a or the related problem of...
- the related question or issue of...
- a related development
- ...bears or bore no relation to...
- the or a relationship between...
- There is a strong relationship between...
- Closely related to...is or are...
- is or are closely associated with...
- akin to...
- ...should be seen in *context*
- a combination of...and...
- ..., combined with
- ...associated with...
- ...in association with...
- ...is strongly linked to...
- *contact* between...and...
- the interplay of or between...
- ...goes hand in hand with...
- ...and...act in concert
- an *integral* part of...
- a *network* of...

Agreement and correspondence

- ...agrees with...
- There is general or *widespread* agreement on or that...
- ...coincides with...
- ...corresponds to...
- the or a correspondence between...
- a *corresponding*...
- Correspondingly,...

Comparing and contrasting

- This shows that the correspondence or relationship between…and…is not necessarily a simple one.
- …and…*overlap*
- complementary
- …and vice versa

Contrast

- in *contrast* to…
- …contrasts with…
- …is in stark *contrast* to or with…
- a marked *contrast*
- In or by *contrast*,…
- *Conversely*,…
- …, *whereas*…
- on the *contrary*,…
- the *reverse* is actually the case
- …contradicts…
- …is contradicted by…
- contradicting theories or *research*
- …contains a number of contradictions
- *Contrary* to expectations,…
- *Paradoxically*,…
- …*versus*…
- …and…are *incompatible*
- a *conflict* between…and…
- the opposite of…
- opposite to…
- as opposed to…
- juxtaposition of…and…

Difference

- …differ in a number of respects
- …differs considerably from…
- …differs significantly from…
- …is or are markedly different from or to…
- …differs slightly from…
- …differs only in small respects from…
- an important difference or *distinction*
- though the similarity is clear, there is a *crucial* or an important difference
- There is a *fundamental* difference between…
- There are a number of important differences, not only in…, but also…
- What differentiates…is…
- a *distinction* between…and…
- to make or draw a *distinction* between…
- A *distinction* must be made between…
- It is important to distinguish between…
- This *distinction* is important, because…
- *Differentiation* of…is important for two etc. reasons
- *maintenance* of this *distinction* is important because…
- …poses different problems to…
- to differentiate…
- …is not *consistent* with…
- this is not the case for…
- the same is not true for…
- the analogy does not hold for…
- this *parallel* does not, however, extend to…
- The disparity between the results may be due to…
- The discrepancy between…and…may be explained by…
- …deviates from…
- …diverge considerably or widely
- diverging views of…
- unlike…
- …not necessarily *identical* or the same
- Some…, while or *whereas* others…
- …runs counter to…
- …at odds with current theories of…

Comparing and contrasting

- the dividing line between…and…
- the dichotomy of or between…and…
- …and…are mutually exclusive

> **Writing practice 24: Comparing and contrasting**
>
> 1. Using phrases from the section above, compare and contrast parts of your text. Discuss
> a. How they are similar
> b. How they differ
>
> 2. Using the words in italics in the section above, write five new phrases for your text
>
> 3. In class, in groups or in pairs, exchange texts and evaluate each other's writing, going through the points above

25 Tying a text or presentation together

> *Science is built up of facts, as a house is built of stones;*
> *but an accumulation of facts is not more a science than a heap of stones is a house*
> Henri Poincaré

The phrases in this section help you tie your paper or presentation together. This makes your work more coherent and helps your reader or audience grasp your overall idea.

- this study
- the present paper or article
- …, including…
- both…and…
- together with…
- throughout this study
- (a), (b), (c)…
- (i), (ii), (iii)…

- Firstly, secondly, thirdly etc.…
- Firstly,…, followed by…, and finally…
- In part 1,…; in part 2,…; and in part 3…
- on page X
- in the *paragraph* above or below
- in the *section* above or below
- in *chapter* X
- in chapters X–X above or below

■ Tying a text or presentation together

Referring forwards

- below
- ...as follows:
- followed by...
- In addition,...
- *Furthermore*,...
- Moreover,...
- Accordingly,...
- By implication,...
- Similarly,...
- Equally,...
- A further point is...
- A further argument is...
- a related development
- the related question or issue of...
- As well as...,...also occurs...
- Also, there is or are...
- In a *similar* vein,...
- Building on...,...
- Alternatively,...
- This brings us to the question of...
- We now turn to...
- Now consider the issue of...
- Next...
- The next *section*...
- in the next *chapter* or *section*
- as discussed in the next *chapter*
- The next *section* introduces...
- The following *chapter* addresses...
- The next *section* broadens the discussion to include...
- The next *section* takes up a number of *issues* raised in this discussion.
- It will be shown in *chapter* X that or how...
- As will be discussed or shown or seen further below,...
- ...is or are discussed further below

- ..., as will be outlined later in the paper,...
- ..., about which more below
- ...(discussed below)
- ..., which will be taken up in *chapter* X
- ...will be discussed in detail in *chapter* X
- ...will be discussed in *subsequent* sections
- ...will be shown both in this and in *subsequent* chapters
- ...will be dealt with or discussed or taken up in the following sections
- The relevance of...to...will be discussed in...
- The relevance of...to...is discussed further or in detail in X.X.
- for reasons discussed below
- in the sense described or discussed above
- Reasons for this are discussed later in the *chapter*.
- in the remainder of the paper

Referring back

- above
- in the last *section*
- at the beginning of the paper or *chapter*
- To summarize:
- To *sum* up:
- To recap:
- as already noted
- as already mentioned
- as already stated
- as shown above
- as already discussed
- as stated or discussed or described in...

Tying a text or presentation together

- as stated or discussed or described above
- ...of the kind or type described or discussed above
- for reasons discussed above
- as a result of the *factors* discussed in...
- the points discussed above
- ...has already been pointed out above
- ...has already been referred to or touched on earlier
- It was noted earlier or above that or how...
- Returning to the example of...,...
- This type of development etc. has already been referred to in *chapter* X
- the discussion above has argued...
- the discussion so far has concentrated on...
- the *preceding* discussion has shown how...
- ..., which has been shown to...
- We have previously shown how...
- The discussion above demonstrates clearly...
- From the *preceding* discussion it is clear that...
- Given the...discussed or described above,...
- In view of this,...
- As a result,...
- So far, I have not commented on...

Writing practice 25: Tying a text or presentation together

1. Using phrases from the section above, tie your text or presentation together, making it more coherent
a. Guide your reader or audience through your argument, referring forwards or back in your text or talk

2. Using the words in italics in the section above, write five new phrases for your text or talk

3. In class, in groups or in pairs, evaluate each other's writing or presentations, going through the points above

26 Presenting results

Certain people – men, of course – discouraged me, saying [science] was not a good career for women. That pushed me even more to persevere
Francoise Barré-Sinoussi

The phrases below help you present your results – both positive results and negative ones.

- The results of…
- …are given below:
- …are shown in table X
- …are *illustrated* by figure X
- …are shown in the graph above or below
- …are given in the *appendix*
- Figure X shows the *distribution* of…
- the outcome of the experiment
- The result that emerges from…is…
- the resulting…
- we *detected*…
- the *output* varies depending on…
- …*generated* the following results…
- The *analysis* or experiment etc. yielded *data* on…
- …was more pronounced…
- …typically increased by or to…
- …typically decreased by or to…
- …under these conditions…
- …occurred in spite of…
- …took place even though…
- …is found even in cases where…
- The *proportion* of…ranged from…to…
- The effects of…on…were greatest in…
- The observed…is or was lower or higher than *predicted*.
- The results of…
- …suggest that…
- …appear to confirm…

- …show a clear pattern
- …fall within a narrow *range*
- …show wide variation
- …clearly *demonstrate*…
- …provide definitive *evidence* of or for…
- …prove…
- …disprove the *theory* or *hypothesis* or claim that…
- …cast doubt on earlier findings…
- Typically,…
- a *major* feature of…
- a clear-cut case of…
- The *evidence* suggests that…
- …results from…
- …affected primarily…
- the effect of…is…
- the presence of…usually indicates…
- absence of…suggests that…
- this in part reflects…
- …was or were found to have…
- …was or were shown to have…
- …resulted in a characteristic…
- …was particularly noticeable
- …was completely successful in…
- …was partially successful in…
- a borderline case
- borderline indices
- …are or were *ambiguous*
- …are or were inconclusive

Presenting results

- The main point is…
- Based on these results,…
- without jumping to conclusions
- The investigations reveal that…
- It is perhaps not surprising that…
- This is an interesting finding because it…
- There are a number of points worth noting or stressing
- The study has *identified* a number of general trends
- The results lend strong support to the argument that…
- A number of *issues* have been resolved
- A number of…are worth examining more closely.

Negative results

- The results of…were negative
- We did not find…
- There was little or no change in…
- There was little improvement in…
- There was little correlation between…
- There was no detectable increase etc. in…
- No effect of…on…was observed
- …could not be *identified*
- …was not *significant*

- …remained *constant*
- …did not increase the…
- …did or does not significantly *affect*…
- …was or were unaffected by…
- …had little or no effect on…
- the effect of…on…was *minimal*
- …had little *impact* on…
- …did not vary greatly with…
- …did not change or *alter* etc. significantly
- …showed no *significant* change in…
- …is unlikely to have affected…
- …is unlikely to have been affected by…
- …was adversely affected by…
- …was unsuccessful in…
- We *encountered* a number of difficulties or problems
- the failure of…
- …failed to…
- The results are somewhat *distorted* by…
- only half of…
- over half of…
- Of a total of…, only…
- …where information was *available*…
- …for whom information was *available*…
- *Individual* results vary; however,…
- The experiments yielded conflicting *data* on…

Writing practice 26: Presenting results

1. Using the phrases above, present your results
   a. Also discuss any negative findings
2. Write and present a poster on your work, either individually or in groups or pairs
3. Using the words in italics in the section above, write five new phrases for your text
4. In class, in groups or in pairs, exchange texts and evaluate each other's writing, going through the points above

Interpreting findings

27 Interpreting findings

*Millions saw the apple fall,
Newton was the only one who asked why*
Bernard M. Baruch

Use the phrases in this section to discuss your findings: whether they agree with other research, and findings that are unexpected or contradict previous studies.

- The findings etc. discussed here are from…
- This means that…
- It is clear that…
- The *statistics* show clearly that…
- It is *significant* that…
- Significantly,…
- Most significantly,…
- …plays a *major role* in…
- an important point
- a *fundamental* factor
- the main cause of…is…
- This raises a number of questions
- It is probable that…
- It is likely that…
- It seems clear that…
- …can be *attributed* to…
- This suggests that…
- This indicates that…
- This or the *evidence* points to…as a factor in…
- The findings *indicate* that…
- The *data* suggest that…
- This seems to *indicate* that…
- …, which indicates or suggests or confirms…
- …, indicating or suggesting or confirming that…

- It is possible that…
- this may be due to…
- It is possible to speculate…
- One may speculate whether…
- It can hardly be a coincidence that…
- *preliminary evidence* suggests that…
- The *preliminary* findings suggest…
- There are a number of *factors* or points worth noting:
- The results suggest that…is due to…rather than…
- The significance of…as a factor *in*…is suggested by…
- The benefits of this approach are immediately *visible*
- The existence of…may be *illustrated* by…
- The influence of…on…is indisputable
- This means that we are able to *link*…and…
- It is important to distinguish carefully between…
- It is important to emphasize…
- Here we see an example of the importance of…
- This underlines the importance of…
- It is perhaps not surprising that…

Interpreting findings

- An interesting aspect of…that emerges is…
- given the findings etc. discussed or described above
- Given…, it is possible to propose or state that…
- It is uncertain whether…
- One *interpretation* of *this* would be…
- One *reading* of *this* would be…
- One way of interpreting…
- Turning this around, we can say that…
- It is important not to overlook…
- There are systematic differences in…
- …is not primarily governed or determined by…, but by…
- The *consequences* of this are…
- One of the most *obvious consequences* of…is…
- A further important consequence of…is that…
- …may have a number of *implications* for…
- …has or have important *implications* for…
- A further implication of…is that…

Agreement

- Taken together,…
- *Similar* results were or have been *obtained* by…
- *Similar* results are found in…, suggesting that…
- The results *coincide* with those of X
- This finding is *consistent* with…
- The results are *consistent* with…
- As *predicted*,…
- as *predicted* by the model

- …shows or showed *evidence* of…
- there is limited *evidence* of…
- The findings etc. provide conclusive support for…
- this has *reinforced* our view that…
- Many of our or the findings confirm…found by X
- The results closely match those *obtained* by X
- The results generally agree with those *obtained* in *previous* studies.
- The results agree by and large with those reported in a study of…by X.

Contradictory, unexpected or inconclusive findings

- Surprisingly,…
- Unexpectedly,…
- *Contrary* to expectations,…
- The results of…were unexpected.
- The most striking finding is that…
- The results *contrast* with X who found…
- There is or was little *evidence* to suggest that…
- There is or was little *evidence* to support…
- There is or was little *evidence* of…
- …is or was not corroborated by the *evidence*…
- There was no *evidence* of…
- This does not imply that…
- The results of…do not support the *hypothesis* of or that…
- The results of…invalidate the *hypothesis* of or that…
- The results suggest, *contrary* to current *theory*, that…

Interpreting findings

- The results call for some explanation and comment:...
- A number of *elements* require further explanation
- This surprising result may be due to...
- It is not clear why...
- It is not immediately *obvious* how or why...
- ...may have been indirectly influenced by...
- although the *mechanism* is not completely understood
- The results are unclear or inconclusive or contradictory
- ...can be interpreted in a number of ways
- The *impact* of...on...is not easy to determine
- The *data* cannot adequately explain...
- ...complicates the *assessment* of the *data*
- *Interpretation* of the *data* is complicated by...
- The results are to some extent misleading
- The results must be interpreted with a degree of or the utmost caution
- The findings are not *consistent* with...
- The disparity between the results may be due to...
- These disparities may reflect...
- The discrepancy between...may be explained by...
- These *apparent* differences may be explained by...
- While it may seem unlikely that..., it is important to remember that...
- The reasons for...remain unclear.

Writing practice 27: Interpreting findings

1. Using phrases from the section above, interpret your findings

a. Discuss findings that confirm or agree with your hypothesis or argument

b. Discuss contradictory, unexpected or inconclusive findings

2. Using the words in italics in the section above, write five new phrases for your text or talk

3. In class, in groups or in pairs, evaluate each other's writing or presentations, going through the points above

28 Concluding a study or presentation

*To myself I am only a child playing on the beach,
while vast oceans of truth lie undiscovered before me*
Isaac Newton

In your conclusions, you should asses your contribution and discuss the limitations of your study. You should then write about any implications or applications of your work, and make suggestions or recommendations for future studies.

- In *conclusion*,…
- To conclude:
- Finally,…
- we are able to draw a number of conclusions
- Concluding this *section*, we can say that…
- From this, we can draw several conclusions:
- We can conclude from the *data* that…
- Concluding this *section*, it may be argued that…
- it is reasonable to conclude that…
- One *conclusion* might be that…
- a number of tentative conclusions can be drawn:
- However, it would be rash to conclude that…
- The answer etc. probably lies somewhere between these two poles.

Contribution

- This study, *thesis*, paper etc.
- …has attempted to…
- …has shown or demonstrated…
- …has focused attention on…
- …may stimulate the *debate* on…
- …extends *previous* work on…
- …has put forward an explanation of or for…
- …has put forward a tentative explanation of or for…
- …has provided *evidence* of or for…
- …has provided convincing or conclusive *evidence* of or for…
- …has provided conclusive support for…
- …has provided *empirical* validation of or for…
- …has made a *contribution* towards…
- …contributes to our understanding of…
- …may contribute towards a better understanding of…
- …has gone some way towards understanding or explaining…
- …has been able to make a number of generalizations about…
- …differs from *previous research* in a number of respects
- …differs from *previous research* in that…
- …offers an *alternative* view or *interpretation* of…
- …has *highlighted* a number of problems with or in…

Concluding a study or presentation

- …has drawn attention to a number of problem areas in existing *theory*
- To our knowledge, this is the first examination of…
- This, to our knowledge, is the first study to…
- This *approach* etc.
- …has enabled better explanation of…
- …has enabled *underlying* principles to be *identified* more clearly
- we were or have been able to *link*…and…
- an explanation for…
- a key insight into…
- …is a new and interesting observation
- the *theory* developed in this study
- This underlines the importance of…
- The advantages of this *approach* are…
- It is clear from the current study that…
- a number of tentative conclusions on…
- A number of key *issues* have been addressed in this study.
- One of the most important contributions of this study is…
- …represents one of the main contributions of this study
- …*identified* by the *investigation*
- …*identified* in the study
- We were able to *document* a number of cases of…
- The results *exceed* those previously achieved
- The results suggest, *contrary* to current *theory*, that…
- In *contrast* to *previous research* on…, this study has attempted to…

- Developments viewed in isolation by earlier studies are here considered together.

Limitations

- A or one *significant* problem is…
- …is a serious obstacle to…
- The problem is a *complex* one.
- There are *obvious* limitations to or in…
- …can only be *adequately* explained by…
- …is beyond the *scope* of this study
- whether…also applies to…is unclear
- the *precise* or exact *mechanism* for or of…remains unclear
- practical *implementation* of…poses a number of problems
- The question remains, however,…
- What the study is unable to say is…
- This study does not claim to be able to…
- It would be rash to conclude from this that…
- It is *still* uncertain whether…
- …remains an open question
- It remains to be seen whether…
- It would be unwise at present to…
- *Nevertheless*, it must be emphasized that…
- We should *stress* that these results are only provisional.
- As with all such studies, there are limitations that offer opportunities for further *research*.
- further work or *research* is *required* in order to…
- further work or *research* is necessary before we can…
- much work remains to be done on…

Concluding a study or presentation

- ...requires a great deal of further *research*
- ...remains a *considerable challenge* to or for...
- At present, these or such *goals* seem remote.

Implications and applications

- This *implies* that...
- This may well imply that...
- It may well be that...
- The results or findings or conclusions presented here...
- ...can also be applied to...
- ...may be applicable to...
- ...may be *relevant* to...
- ...may be *significant* in...
- ...may be of practical importance in or to...
- ...may have important *implications* for...
- ...may have a number of *implications* for...
- ...may have wider *implications* for...
- ...may have wider relevance to...
- A number of the conclusions of the study may be valid for...
- A number of the conclusions of this study may have wider *validity* to...
- In practical terms,...
- the theoretical or practical *implications* of...
- a number of important or practical applications
- One application of...is...
- In the light of these results,...
- ...suggests some common *factors*
- whether or not...is or are also applicable to...
- if the results are reproducible in other studies, contexts etc.
- One question is to what extent the conclusions of this study may be applicable to...
- The results of this study suggest a number of new avenues for *research*
- The findings presented here provide a starting point for further examination or *investigation* of...
- This study raises a number of questions concerning or about...

Suggestions and recommendations

- ...is needed
- ...is necessary
- ...is *required*
- a new *approach*
- One strategy would be to...
- an *emphasis* not on..., but on...
- This highlights the importance of...
- ...may be important in re-examining...
- ...is or are worth exploring further
- The problem merits further *investigation*.
- The *challenge* for future *research* or studies will be to...
- Clearly, further *research* is necessary before...
- This demonstrates or shows or makes clear the need for...
- The questions raised by this study warrant further *investigation*.
- Any model of...which does not take...into account is by *definition* incomplete

Concluding a study or presentation

- This emphasizes or underlines the need for…
- A study of…must take account of…
- Other authors have also called for…
- Unless we…, we are at risk of…
- …we run the risk of…
- re-examine our foundations
- The aim of *research* on…must surely be…

Writing practice 28: Concluding a study or presentation

1. Using phrases from the section above, write a conclusion to your text or presentation

a. Discuss what your text or talk contributes

b. Discuss its limitations

c. Discuss any implications or applications arising from your work

d. Give recommendations for future study

2. Using the words in italics in the section above, write five new phrases for your text or talk

3. In class, in groups or in pairs, evaluate each other's writing or presentations, going through the points above

29 Summary and abstract

*Discovery consists of seeing what everybody has seen
and thinking what nobody has thought*
Albert von Szent-Györgyi

A summary or abstract is a short text giving the main points of your paper or presentation.

- *Overall*,…
- On balance,…
- Briefly,…
- In short,…
- Essentially,…
- an overview of…
- a *brief* outline of…
- a *brief* account of…is given below etc.
- To summarize:
- In *summary*, we have shown that…
- In *summary*, we can state that…
- …can be summarized as follows:
- The main points are:
- there are a number of points worth reiterating:
- The discussion so far has focused on…
- In this *section*,…was presented
- The purpose of this *section* has been to…
- We have *sought* to explain or clarify…
- It has been shown in this *chapter*…
- The effects of…on…were studied in…
- This study has shown…
- This study has attempted to…
- The study represents a first or *initial* attempt at or to…
- In this study, we have investigated or examined…
- A main point of this study has been to…
- It is the central argument of this study that…
- *Chapter* X draws together the main findings of the study.
- One of the most important findings of this study is…

Book jackets

- This study examines…
- This *volume* for the first time…
- This book is an introduction to…
- a *comprehensive* introduction to…
- an overview of…
- a revised *edition* of…
- a thoroughly revised *edition* of…
- a completely revised and updated *edition* of…
- a textbook
- a valuable teaching *aid*
- a useful reference for…
- It includes an extensive bibliography of…
- Since its first *publication* in…,…
- X's widely acclaimed book etc. on…
- The new *edition*…
- In this work,…
- It covers…
- It surveys the…
- Areas covered include…

Summary and abstract

- *Issues* addressed in this *volume* include…
- Topics discussed include…
- It investigates how and why…
- In this *volume*, X provides…
- …, and draws on *data* from…
- a wide-ranging discussion
- …, giving special attention to…
- It takes into account recent *research* on…
- It incorporates the latest developments in…
- incorporating recent developments in the field
- …addresses many of the *issues* currently under discussion
- This book will be of particular interest to…
- …will prove invaluable for…
- This book will also be of interest to…
- Although intended primarily for or as…, the book will also be of use to…

Writing practice 29: Summary and abstract

1. Write a summary of your text or presentation

a. Read your whole text, highlighting the most important points

b. From these, write your summary

2. Select a journal in your subject and read its guidelines for abstracts

a. Write an abstract of your text following the journal's guidelines

3. Produce a short text for the jacket of your next book!

4. In class, in groups or in pairs, exchange texts and evaluate each other's writing, going through the points above

30 Making a presentation

The guest will judge better of a feast than the cook
Aristotle

Academic advice: Making a presentation

1. Talk to your audience – don't read
a. Spoken academic English is less formal than written academic English. The phrases in this section are therefore in a more colloquial style appropriate for a presentation.
2. Give an introduction, telling your audience what you will talk about
3. Use a contents slide to show the structure of your talk
a. Repeat this slide at the beginning of each section of your presentation
b. Use a different color for the section slide to make it stand out clearly
4. When you move from one section to the next, pause and tell the audience
5. Watch your timing – keep to the allotted time
a. Speak slowly and pace your presentation
6. Don't fill each slide with too much text
7. Use color to highlight important parts of your slides
a. Use examples and diagrams to help make your point
b. Use images to make your presentation visually stimulating
8. Use rhetorical questions to engage your audience
9. Give a summary, highlighting your main points
10. Practice makes perfect – rehearse your presentation beforehand

Opening your presentation

- Hello everyone
- My name is…
- I'm from…University etc.

Introducing your topic

- My talk today is about…
- In this presentation, I'm going to talk about…

Making a presentation

Explaining the structure of your presentation

- This talk is divided into three etc. parts
- First, I will talk about…
- Then I will discuss or look at…
- Finally, I will…

Referring to the screen, handout or poster

- This slide shows…
- Please look at…
- This shows…
- The table or graph or image shows…

Technical glitches

- I'm sorry, I seem to be having a technical problem. Please bear with me for a moment.
- My apologies for the technical glitch.
- I will move on.

Giving examples

- We can illustrate this with the following example
- The following example shows or demonstrates that…

Linking

- Let's now look at…
- Let's look a little more closely at…
- Let's look at this in a little more detail
- In the next slide,…
- So far, I have looked at…
- I will now look at…

Summarizing

- In this presentation, I have talked about…
- First, I discussed…
- I then talked about…
- Finally, I showed how or that…
- In conclusion, we can state the following:

Closing

- Thank you for listening to my presentation.

Answering questions

- If you have any questions or comments, please feel free to ask.
- I'm sorry, I didn't catch that. Could you repeat the question, please.
- I can see your point, but…
- I'm afraid I don't have the answer to that. If you leave me your contact information, I will get back to you.

Commenting on a presentation

- Thank you for an interesting presentation.
- I enjoyed your presentation very much.
- I wonder if I could ask a couple of questions?
- I have one question and a comment.
- On slide X, you discuss…
- What do you mean by…?
- I didn't quite understand your point on slide X. Could you go over it again?
- Have you read the recent paper or book by X on…
- I wonder if you have considered the possibility that…?

Making a presentation

Writing practice 30: Making a presentation

1. Using phrases from the section above, make a presentation on your topic
a. Present it to your class
b. Listen to their questions and feedback

2. Do your presentation one more time, taking account of the advice of your teacher or audience

3. Video yourself making your presentation
a. Study the video to improve your presentation skills

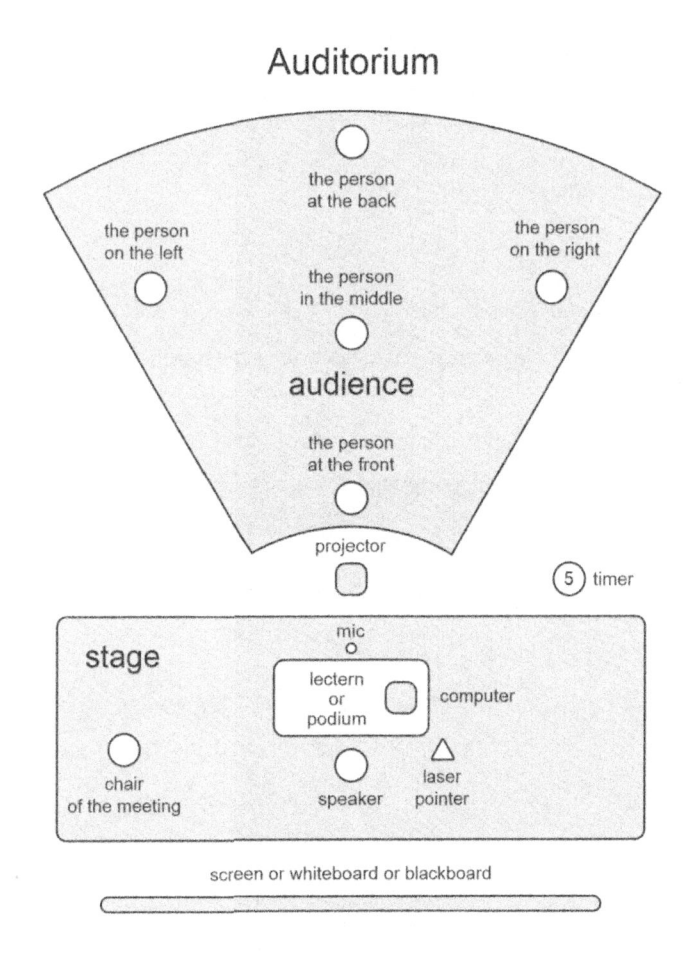

Auditorium

- the person at the back
- the person on the left
- the person in the middle
- the person on the right
- the person at the front

audience

projector

5 timer

stage

mic
lectern or podium
computer
chair of the meeting
speaker
laser pointer

screen or whiteboard or blackboard

■ Writing academic emails

31 Writing academic emails

Ask the right questions,
and nature will open the doors to her secrets
C V Raman

When writing an email, it is important to get the level of formality right. That is not easy, as the level of formality in academia and society varies from country to country. Three important things to take into account when writing academic emails are:

- Whether you know your addressee well
- Your addressee's age compared to your age
- Your addressee's status compared to your status

This section helps you write both formal and polite informal emails in appropriate English. If the status or age gap between you and your addressee is significant, use formal style unless you know her or him well.

Formal email to someone you do not know well

For example, a professor at another institute

Remember to add your contact information if you are writing to someone you do not know well.

Formal email

Subject: Brief, clear subject

Dear Dr Darwin

Main body of email

In a formal email, you can use many of the phrases in this PhraseBook.

Sincerely

Alfred Wallace

Writing academic emails

Formal greeting

- Dear Professor *Family Name*
- Dear Dr *Family Name*

Introducing yourself

- My name is *Full Name*.
- I am an undergraduate student, graduate student or assistant professor in the Department of …at…University.
- My professor or supervisor is *Full Name*.
- I was referred to you by my professor, supervisor, colleague etc., X
- Perhaps you remember that we met at X Conference in Place last year?

Formal main body

- Please accept my apologies for contacting you by email.
- I recently read your paper in…Journal.
- I recently read your study on…
- I am researching or working on…
- I am writing to ask you…
- I wonder whether it would be possible to…
- I would be most grateful for your assistance.
- Please accept my apologies for the bothersome request.

Attachments

- I have taken the liberty of attaching a copy of my paper, thesis etc.

Formal closing

- Sincerely US
- Yours sincerely GB

Informal but polite email to someone you know well

For example, a colleague of similar age and status

Informal email
Subject: Brief, clear subject
Hi Charles
Main body of email
In an informal email, you can use contracted forms such as *I've*, *don't*, *isn't* etc.
Best regards
Alfred

Writing academic emails

Informal greeting

- Hi *Given Name*
- Hello *Given Name*

Informal main body

- I hope you are well.
- Thank you for your email yesterday or last week.
- I'm sorry for my late reply.
- Perhaps you remember that we spoke last week *etc.* about…
- I'm sorry to bother you, but…
- I wonder if I could ask you…
- I wonder whether you could…
- I wonder if we could meet next week *etc.*?
- I wonder whether you would have time to read through my paper or thesis this week *etc.*?
- I'd be really grateful for your help.
- I'm sorry to bother you while you are busy.

Attachments

- I have attached a copy of my paper, chapter, thesis *etc.*

Informal closing

- Best wishes
- Best regards

Writing practice 31: Writing academic emails

1. Using phrases from the section above, write a formal email asking a professor at another university for help with your research
2. Write an informal email to your classmate asking for help with your studies
3. In class, in groups or in pairs, exchange emails and evaluate each other's writing, going through the points above

Printed in Great Britain
by Amazon